CW01425501

Arduino Meets MATLAB Interfacing, Programs and Simulink

Authored by:

Rajesh Singh

*School of Electronics & Electrical Engineering, Lovely Professional University
Jalandhar, Punjab, India*

Anita Gehlot

*School of Electronics & Electrical Engineering, Lovely Professional University
Jalandhar, Punjab, India*

Bhupendra Singh

Schematics Microelectronics, Dehradun, Uttrakhand, India

&

Sushabhan Choudhury

*Department of Electronics & Electrical Engineering, University of Petroleum
and Energy Studies, Dehradun, Uttrakhand, India*

Arduino Meets MATLAB: Interfacing, Programs and Simulink

Authors: Rajesh Singh, Anita Gehlot, Bhupendra Singh, Sushabhan Choudhury

ISBN (Online): 978-1-68108-727-6

ISBN (Print): 978-1-68108-728-3

© 2018, Bentham eBooks imprint.

Published by Bentham Science Publishers – Sharjah, UAE. All Rights Reserved.

BENTHAM SCIENCE PUBLISHERS LTD.
End User License Agreement (for non-institutional, personal use)

This is an agreement between you and Bentham Science Publishers Ltd. Please read this License Agreement carefully before using the ebook/echapter/ejournal (**"Work"**). Your use of the Work constitutes your agreement to the terms and conditions set forth in this License Agreement. If you do not agree to these terms and conditions then you should not use the Work.

Bentham Science Publishers agrees to grant you a non-exclusive, non-transferable limited license to use the Work subject to and in accordance with the following terms and conditions. This License Agreement is for non-library, personal use only. For a library / institutional / multi user license in respect of the Work, please contact: permission@benthamscience.org.

Usage Rules:

1. All rights reserved: The Work is the subject of copyright and Bentham Science Publishers either owns the Work (and the copyright in it) or is licensed to distribute the Work. You shall not copy, reproduce, modify, remove, delete, augment, add to, publish, transmit, sell, resell, create derivative works from, or in any way exploit the Work or make the Work available for others to do any of the same, in any form or by any means, in whole or in part, in each case without the prior written permission of Bentham Science Publishers, unless stated otherwise in this License Agreement.
2. You may download a copy of the Work on one occasion to one personal computer (including tablet, laptop, desktop, or other such devices). You may make one back-up copy of the Work to avoid losing it. The following DRM (Digital Rights Management) policy may also be applicable to the Work at Bentham Science Publishers' election, acting in its sole discretion:

- 25 'copy' commands can be executed every 7 days in respect of the Work. The text selected for copying cannot extend to more than a single page. Each time a text 'copy' command is executed, irrespective of whether the text selection is made from within one page or from separate pages, it will be considered as a separate / individual 'copy' command.
- 25 pages only from the Work can be printed every 7 days.

3. The unauthorised use or distribution of copyrighted or other proprietary content is illegal and could subject you to liability for substantial money damages. You will be liable for any damage resulting from your misuse of the Work or any violation of this License Agreement, including any infringement by you of copyrights or proprietary rights.

Disclaimer:

Bentham Science Publishers does not guarantee that the information in the Work is error-free, or warrant that it will meet your requirements or that access to the Work will be uninterrupted or error-free. The Work is provided "as is" without warranty of any kind, either express or implied or statutory, including, without limitation, implied warranties of merchantability and fitness for a particular purpose. The entire risk as to the results and performance of the Work is assumed by you. No responsibility is assumed by Bentham Science Publishers, its staff, editors and/or authors for any injury and/or damage to persons or property as a matter of products liability, negligence or otherwise, or from any use or operation of any methods, products instruction, advertisements or ideas contained in the Work.

Limitation of Liability:

In no event will Bentham Science Publishers, its staff, editors and/or authors, be liable for any damages, including, without limitation, special, incidental and/or consequential damages and/or damages for lost data and/or profits arising out of (whether directly or indirectly) the use or inability to use the Work. The entire liability of Bentham Science Publishers shall be limited to the amount actually paid by you for the Work.

General:

1. Any dispute or claim arising out of or in connection with this License Agreement or the Work (including non-contractual disputes or claims) will be governed by and construed in accordance with the laws of the U.A.E. as applied in the Emirate of Dubai. Each party agrees that the courts of the Emirate of Dubai shall have exclusive jurisdiction to settle any dispute or claim arising out of or in connection with this License Agreement or the Work (including non-contractual disputes or claims).

2. Your rights under this License Agreement will automatically terminate without notice and without the need for a court order if at any point you breach any terms of this License Agreement. In no event will any delay or failure by Bentham Science Publishers in enforcing your compliance with this License Agreement constitute a waiver of any of its rights.

3. You acknowledge that you have read this License Agreement, and agree to be bound by its terms and conditions. To the extent that any other terms and conditions presented on any website of Bentham Science Publishers conflict with, or are inconsistent with, the terms and conditions set out in this License Agreement, you acknowledge that the terms and conditions set out in this License Agreement shall prevail.

Bentham Science Publishers Ltd.
Executive Suite Y - 2
PO Box 7917, Saif Zone
Sharjah, U.A.E.
Email: subscriptions@benthamscience.org

BENTHAM SCIENCE

CONTENTS

FOREWORD

This book titled Arduino meets MATLAB. .. Interfacing, Programs and Simulink will provide a platform for the beginners to get started with Arduino and its interfacing with the MATLAB. The book provides the basic knowledge of the programming and interfacing of the devices with Arduino and MATLAB. This book also explains in a lucid manner the basic steps to understand the interfacing and programming with Arduino and MATLAB. This book goes from basic to advanced level of Arduino and interfacing with various input/output devices through various communication modules in well defined sequence which will be easily understandable to the undergraduate and post graduate students. This book will be specially beneficial to those researchers looking for hardware based implementation platforms.

The USP of this book lies in the fact that a new concept has been introduced for the researchers and students for prototype development of the real time projects using Arduino, MATLAB and I/O devices in the single platform. Another important point to mention will be that this book is entirely based on the practical experience of the authors while undergoing projects with the students and industries.

Dr. Babu Sena Paul
Department of Electrical and Electronic Engineering Technology
University of Johannesburg
South Africa

PREFACE

The primary objective of writing this book is to provide a platform for the beginners to get started with Arduino and its interfacing with the MATLAB. The book provides the basic knowledge of the programming and interfacing of the devices with Arduino and its interfacing with MATLAB.

The aim is to explain the basic steps to understand the interfacing and programming to interface Arduino with MATLAB.

This book provides basics to advanced knowledge of Arduino and its interfacing with input/output devices (display devices, actuators, sensors), communication modules (RF modem, Zigbee) and MATLAB. This would be beneficial for the people who want to get started with hardware based project prototypes. Embedded system based on Arduino with simulation, programming and interfacing with MATLAB all at a single platform. Arduino interfacing with MATLAB with and without I/O packages is included. Basics of the Arduino are covered in section-A, how to interface Arduino with basic input/output devices. Section-B covers Arduino interfacing with MATLAB with I/O package and section-C covers Arduino interfacing with Arduino without I/O package.

The concept which makes this book unique is a book programming and simulation of Arduino and MATLAB based real time project prototypes at a single platform.

This book is entirely based on the practical experience of the authors while undergoing projects with the students and industries. Although the circuits and programs mentioned in the text are tested on real hardware but in case of any mistake we extend our sincere apologies. Any suggestions to improve in the contents of book are always welcome and will be appreciated and acknowledged.

CONSENT FOR PUBLICATION

Not applicable.

CONFLICT OF INTEREST

The author(s) declared no conflict of interest regarding the contents of each of the chapters of this book.

ACKNOWLEDGEMENTS

We acknowledge the support from Nutty Engineer to use its products to demonstrate and explain the working of the systems. We would like to thank BENTHAM SCIENCE for encouraging our idea about this book and the support to manage the project efficiently.

We are grateful to the honorable Chancellor (Lovely Professional University) Ashok Mittal, Mrs. Rashmi Mittal (Pro Chancellor, LPU), Dr. Ramesh Kanwar (Vice Chancellor, LPU), Dr. Loviraj Gupta (Executive Dean, LPU) for their support. We are also thankful to the chancellor (UPES) Dr. S.J Chopra, Dr. Dependra Jha (Vice Chancellor, UPES), Dr. Kamal Bansal (Dean, SoE, UPES), Dr. Piyush Kuchhal (Associate Dean, UPES) and Dr. Suresh Kumar (Director, UPES) for their support and constant encouragement. In addition we are thankful to our family, friends, relatives, colleagues and students for their moral support and blessings.

Rajesh Singh
School of Electronics &
Electrical Engineering,
Lovely Professional University,
Jalandhar, Punjab,
India

Anita Gehlot
School of Electronics &
Electrical Engineering,
Lovely Professional University,
Jalandhar, Punjab,
India

Sushabhan Choudhry
Department of Electronics &
Electrical Engineering,
University of Petroleum and Energy Studies,
Dehradun, Uttrakhand,
India

Bhupendra Singh
Schematics Microelectronics,
Dehradun, Uttrakhand,
India

Arduino Meets MATLAB:
Interfacing, Programs and Simulink

CHAPTER 1

Introduction to Arduino, Arduino IDE and Proteus Software

Abstract: Arduino is an open source platform and easy to use software. The chapter is about to discuss the advantages of Arduino with brief description to each Arduino board including UNO, MEGA and NANO. Arduino Integrated Development Environment is used to write the program for Arduino, this chapter elaborates step to step description of writing and compiling the program. Proteus simulator is also introduced, which is used for checking the feasibility of program and working of the designed system without actual implementation on hardware. Design steps are described for the beginners.

Keywords: Arduino, Arduino IDE, Open Source Platform.

Arduino is a user friendly open-source platform. Arduino has on board microcontroller and IDE is used to program it. As compared to similar platforms it is easy to program and has many advantages over them.

ADVANTAGES

Low Cost - Arduino boards are of relatively low-cost as compared to other microcontroller platforms.

Cross-platform - The Arduino Software (IDE) is compatible with Windows, Macintosh OSX, and Linux operating systems, which most of microcontroller systems are not.

User Friendly - The Arduino Software (IDE) is user friendly and easy-to-use for beginners and much flexibility for skilled programmers.

Open Source - The Arduino is an open source software and can be programmed with C, C++ or AVR-C languages. So a variety of modules can be designed by users.

Arduino platform comprises of a microcontroller. It can be connected to PC *via* a USB cable. It is freely accessible and can be easily downloaded from

Rajesh Singh, Anita Gehlot, Bhupendra Singh & Sushabhan Choudhury
All rights reserved-© 2018 Bentham Science Publishers

http://www.arduino.org/downloads. It can also be modified by the programmer. In the market different versions of Arduino boards are available and depending on the requirement of user.

1.1. ARDUINO UNO

The Arduino/Genuino Uno has on board ATmega328 microcontroller. It has on board six analog input ports (A0-A5). Each pin can operate on 0-5V of voltage. It has 14 digital I/O pins out of which 6 are PWM output, 6 analog inputs, 2 KB SRAM, 1 KB EEPROM and operates at 16 MHz of frequency. Table **1.1** shows the pin description of Arduino UNO. Fig. (**1.1**) shows the Arduino Uno board.

Fig. (1.1). Arduino Uno Board.

Table 1.1. Pin Description of Arduino UNO.

Pin	Description
Vin	The external voltage to the Arduino board.
+5V	Output a regulated 5V
3.3 V	On board 3.3 volt supply
GND	Ground
IOREF	provides the voltage reference and select appropriate power source
Serial	Transmits and receives serial data, Pins: 0(Rx) 1(Tx)
External Interrupts	trigger an interrupt on low value (Pins 2 & 3)
PWM	Provides 8 bit PWM output (pins: 3,5,6,9,10,11)
SPI	Supports SPI communication (Pins: 10(SS), 11(MOSI), 12 (MISO) and 13 (SCK))
LED	LED driven by pin 13
TWI	Supports TWI communication (Pins: A4 (SDA), A5(SCL))

(Table 1.1) cont.....

Pin	Description
AREF	Reference voltage for the analog inputs
Reset	It is used to reset the onboard microcontroller

1.2. ARDUINO MEGA

The Arduino Uno has on board ATmega2560 microcontroller. It has on board 16 analog inputs, 54 digital I/O, USB connection, 4 UART, power jack and reset button. It operates on 16 MHz frequency. The board can be operated with 5-12 volts of external power, if supplied more than this it can damage the board. It has on board 256 KB flash memory, 8 KB SRAM, 4 KB EEPROM. Table **1.2** shows the pin description of Arduino Mega. Fig. (**1.2**) shows the Arduino Mega board.

Fig. (1.2). Arduino Mega Board.

Table 1.2. Pin Description of Arduino Mega.

Pin	Description
Vin	The external voltage to the Arduino board.
+5V	Output a regulated 5V
3.3 V	On board 3.3 volt supply
GND	Ground
IOREF	provides the voltage reference and select appropriate power source
Serial0	Transmits and receives serial data, Pins: 0(Rx) 1(Tx)
Serial1	Transmits and receives serial data, Pins: 19(Rx) 18(Tx)
Serial2	Transmits and receives serial data, Pins: 17(Rx) 16(Tx)

(Table 1.2) cont.....

Pin	Description
External Interrupts	trigger an interrupt on low value (Pins 2 (interrupt 0), 3(interrupt1), 18 (interrupt5), 19(interrupt 4), 20 (interrupt2)
PWM	Provides 8 bit PWM output (pins: 2 to 13 and 44 to 46)
SPI	Supports SPI communication (Pins: 53(SS), 51(MOSI), 50 (MISO) and 52 (SCK))
LED	LED driven by pin 13
TWI	Supports TWI communication (Pins: 20 (SDA), 21(SCL))
AREF	Reference voltage for the analog inputs
Reset	It is used to reset the onboard microcontroller

1.3. ARDUINO NANO

The Arduino/Genuino Nano has on board ATmega328 microcontroller. It has on board 8 analog and 14 digital I/O ports and 6 PWM of 8 bit. Each pin can operate on 0-5V of voltage. It has on board 32 KB flash memory, 2 KB SRAM, 1 KB EEPROM and operates at 16 MHz of frequency. Table **1.3** shows the pin description of Arduino NANO. Fig. (**1.3**) shows the Arduino Nano board.

Table 1.3. Pin Description of Arduino NANO.

Pin	Description
Vin	The external voltage to the Arduino board.
+5V	Output a regulated 5V
3.3 V	On board 3.3 volt supply
GND	Ground
IOREF	provides the voltage reference and select appropriate power source
Serial	Transmits and receives serial data, Pins: 0(Rx) 1(Tx)
External Interrupts	trigger an interrupt on low value (Pins 2 & 3)
PWM	Provides 8 bit PWM output (pins: 3,5,6,9,10,11)
SPI	Supports SPI communication (Pins: 10(SS), 11(MOSI), 12 (MISO) and 13 (SCK))
LED	LED driven by pin 13
I2C	Supports TWI communication (Pins: A4 (SDA), A5(SCL))
AREF	Reference voltage for the analog inputs
Reset	It is used to reset the onboard microcontroller

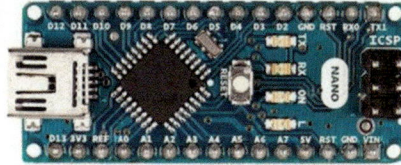

Fig. (1.3). Arduino Nano Board.

1.4. ARDUINO IDE

This section describes the steps to write and compile program with Arduino IDE. The Arduino Integrated Development Environment is open source and it makes it easy to write code and upload it to board.

1.4.1. Steps to Install Arduino IDE

STEP 1: Install Arduino IDE and open the window

To begin, install the Arduino Programmer, the integrated development environment (IDE). Fig. (**1.4**) shows the opened window Arduino IDE.

Fig. (1.4). Window Arduino IDE.

STEP 2: Choose suitable version of Arduino

Arduino has many versions like UNO, MEGA, NANO. The most common is the Arduino UNO. Before start find out the suitable version for the project. Set the board type and the serial port in the Arduino Programmer. To select type of Arduino, Click on "Tool", and then click on "board", Fig. (**1.5**) shows selection of

"Arduino Uno".

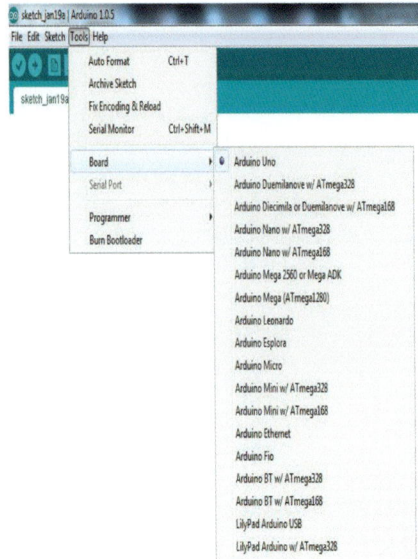

Fig. (1.5). Window to select type of Arduino.

STEP 3: Write and Compile the Program

Write program as per requirement of project. Then "RUN" the program. Fig. (**1.6**) shows the compilation of program.

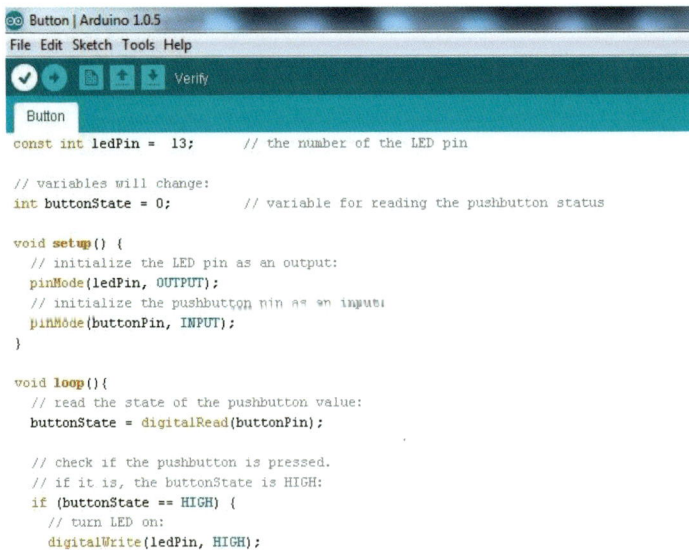

Fig. (1.6). Compile the program.

STEP 4: Connect Arduino with PC

Connect Arduino to the USB port of PC with USB cable. Every Arduino has a different serial-port address (like COM2, COM4 *etc.*), so it is required to reconfigure the port for the different Arduino and select it in IDE. To check the port at which Arduino is connected, make right click on 'PC' then go to manager a window will open. Then double click on 'Device Manager'. A window as shown in Fig. (**1.7**) will open. Click on ports (COM&LPT) and port at which device is connected can be found. Figure shows 'COM6' is port for the device.

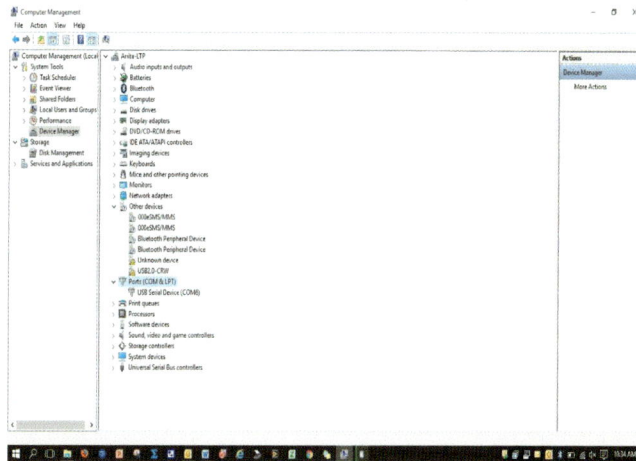

Fig. (1.7). Window to check port of Arduino.

Now click on the 'Tool' heading at Arduino IDE window. Go to port and select the same port no. which was found at device manager (select COM1 or COM2, *etc*). Fig. (**1.8**) shows the 'COM6' as serial port of board.

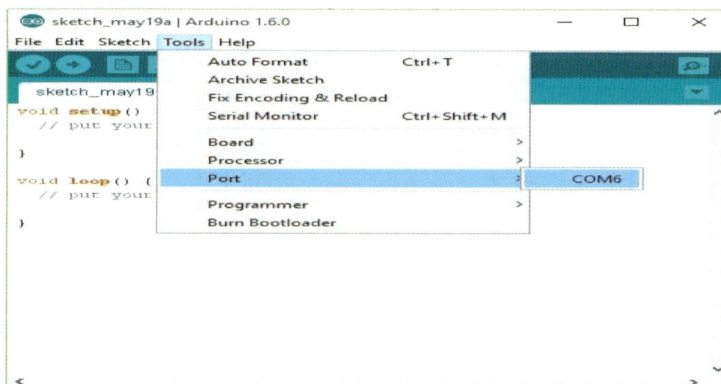

Fig. (1.8). The serial port of board.

STEP 5: Upload program in Arduino

Upload the new program to Arduino. Fig. (**1.9**) shows how to upload program.

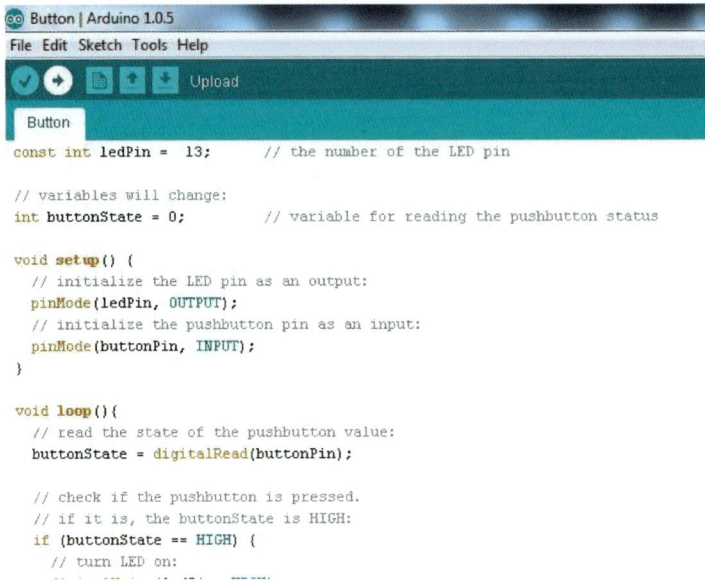

```
Button | Arduino 1.0.5
File  Edit  Sketch  Tools  Help

          Upload

Button

const int ledPin = 13;        // the number of the LED pin

// variables will change:
int buttonState = 0;          // variable for reading the pushbutton status

void setup() {
  // initialize the LED pin as an output:
  pinMode(ledPin, OUTPUT);
  // initialize the pushbutton pin as an input:
  pinMode(buttonPin, INPUT);
}

void loop(){
  // read the state of the pushbutton value:
  buttonState = digitalRead(buttonPin);

  // check if the pushbutton is pressed.
  // if it is, the buttonState is HIGH:
  if (buttonState == HIGH) {
    // turn LED on:
```

Fig. (1.9). Window to upload the program in Arduino.

1.4.2. Basic Commands

1. **pinMode(x, OUTPUT);** //assigned pin number x as output pin where x is number of digital pin
2. **digitalWrite(x, HIGH);** //turn ON the pin number x as HIGH or ON where x is number of digital pin
3. **pinMode(x, INPUT);** //assigned pin number x as input pin where x is number of digital pin
4. **digitalRead(digital Pin);** // read the digital pin like 13 or 12or 11 *etc.*
5. **analogRead(analog pin);** //read the analog pin like A0 or A1 or A2 *etc.*

LCD Commands

1. **lcd.begin(16, 2);** // initialize LCD 16*2 or 20*4
2. **lcd.print("UPES");** // print a string "UPES" on LCD
3. **lcd.setCursor(x, y);** // set the cursor of LCD at desired location where x is number of COLUMN and y
4. **lcd.print(UPES);** // print a UPES as integer on LCD
5. **lcd.Clear();** //clear the contents of LCD

Serial Communication Commands

1. **Serial.begin(baudrate);** //initialize serial communication to set baud rate to 600/1200/2400/ 4800/9600
2. **Serial.print("UPES");** // serial print fixed string with define baud rate on Tx line
3. **Serial.println("UPES");** // serial print fixed string with define baud rate and enter command on Tx line
4. **Serial.print(UPES);** // serial print int string with define baud rate on Tx line
5. **Serial.print(UPES);** // serial print int string with define baud rate and enter command on Tx line
6. **Serial.Write(BYTE);** //serial transfer the one byte on Tx line
7. **Serial.read();** // read one byte serial from Rx line

1.5. INTRODUCTION TO PROTEUS SIMULATION SOFTWARE

Proteus Simulator can be used for microcontroller simulation, schematic capture and printed circuit board (PCB). It is developed by Lab center Electronics. This is a tool for engineers to check the feasibility of the prototype in virtual environment before actual implementation on hardware.

1.5.1. Steps to Design a Proteus Simulation Model

Install ISIS professional on desktop/laptop and make shortcut on desktop for convient use of software.

Step 1- Open ISIS professional. Fig. (**1.10**) shows the ISIS window.

Fig. (**1.10**). Open the ISIS professional.

Step 2- Proteus window will be opened as shown in Fig. (**1.11**) Select 'NO' option for view sample design.

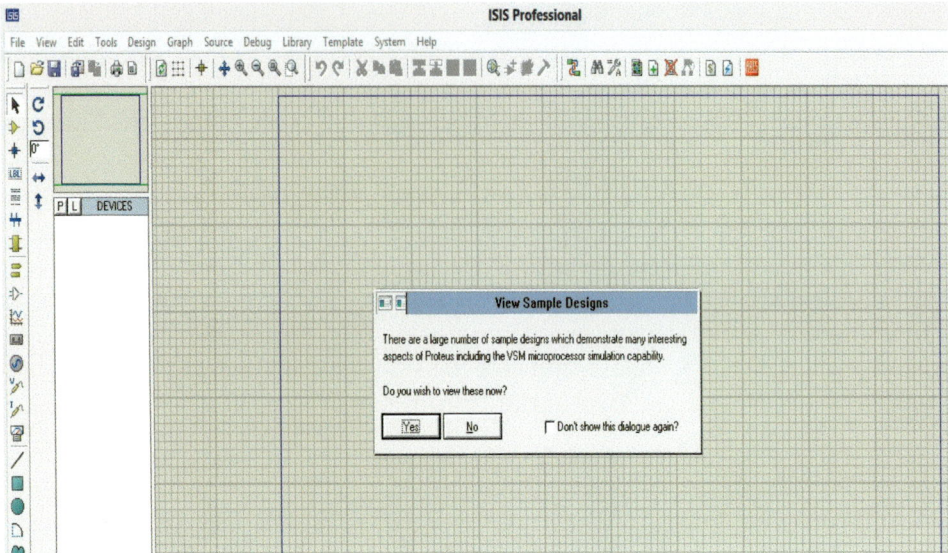

Fig. (1.11). Proteus window.

Step 3- For components selection click on 'P' option at the left side of the window (*i.e.* pick from library) as shown in Fig. (**1.12**).

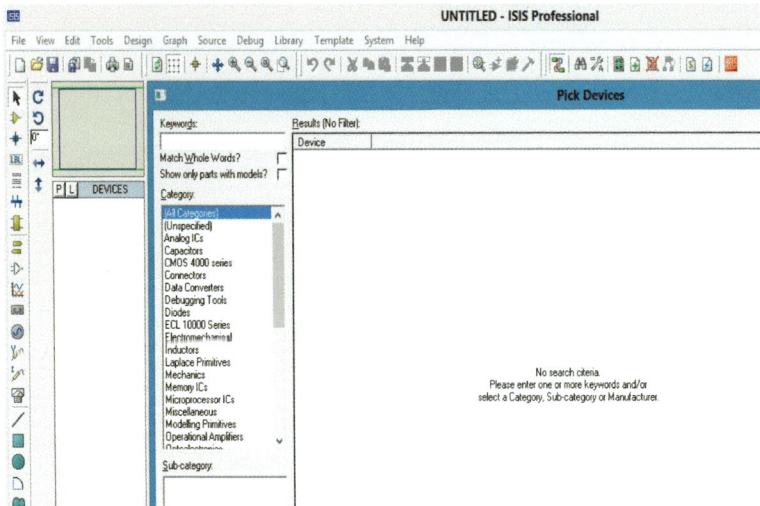

Fig. (1.12). Device selection from library.

Step 4- Library browser will be opened, type the component name in keywords. Make double click on device then it will be added to project device list. Fig. (**1.13**) shows how to add components.

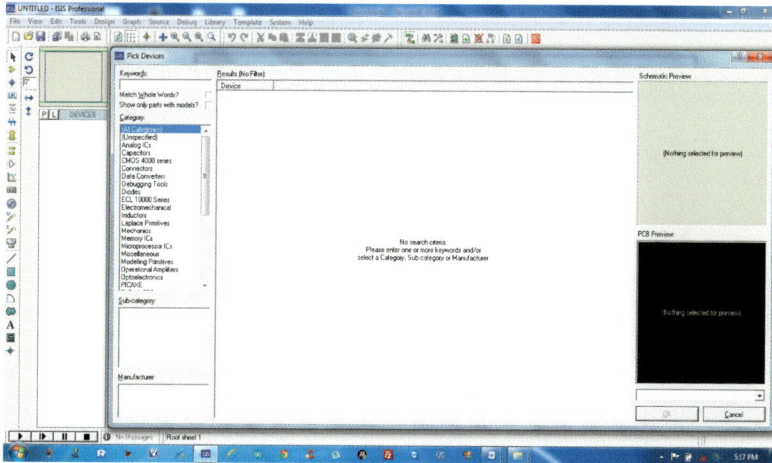

Fig. (1.13). Add the components.

Step 5- To place the component, click on the component and drag it on drawing area. To rotate the component it has options like anticlockwise and clockwise. To move it on area, right click on the component and then click on 'Drag the object'. Fig. (**1.14**) shows selection of components. Fig. (**1.15**) shows how to drag selected components in drawing area.

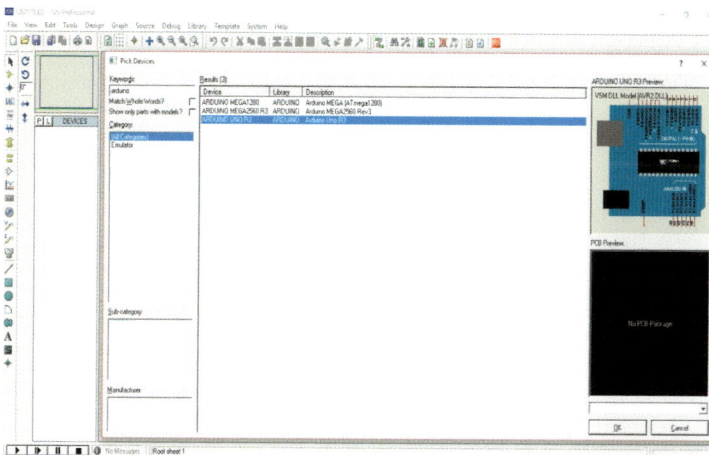

Fig. (1.14). Selection of the component.

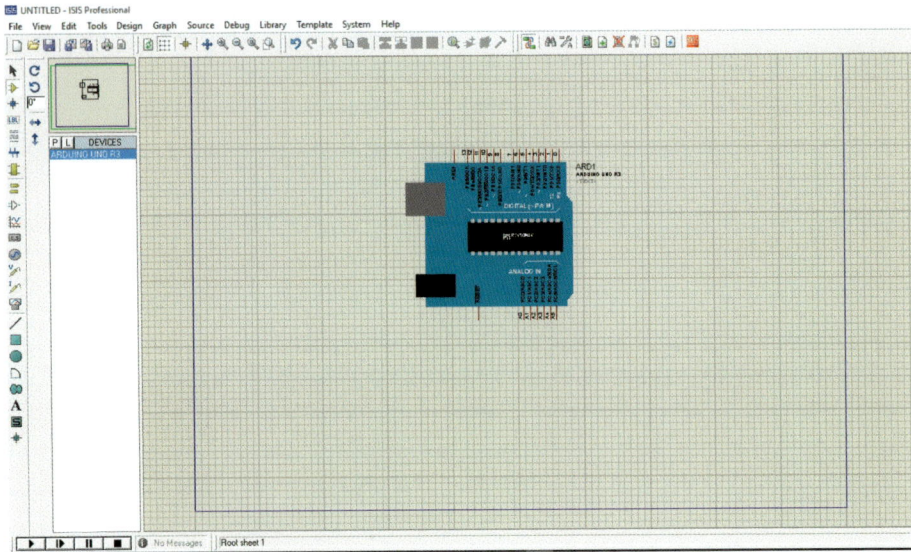

Fig. (1.15). Drag device on drawing area.

Step 6- To connect the components, wire the component by taking the one pin at one end and then click it at the other end (to be connected). Fig. (**1.16**) shows connection of two devices.

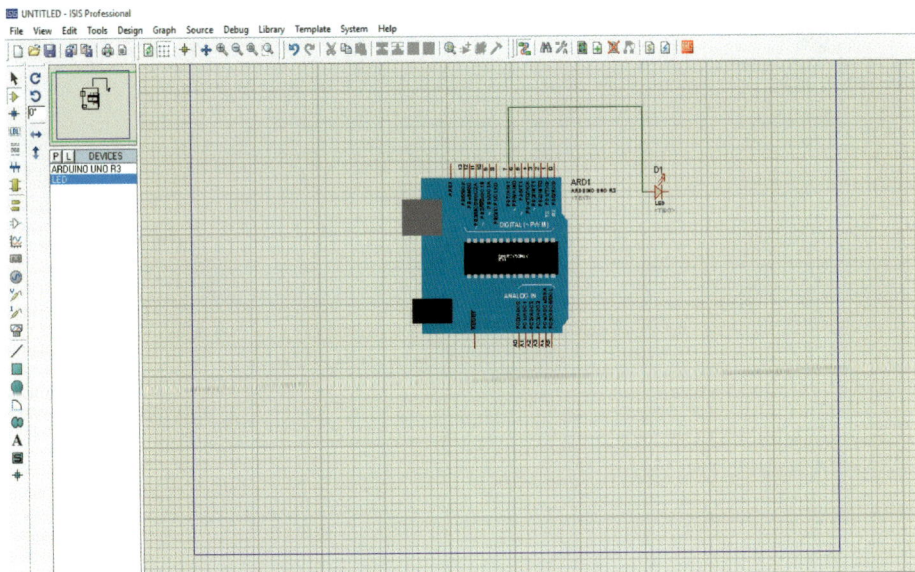

Fig. (1.16). Connecting two devices.

Step 7- After the design is completed save it.

Step 8- To burn the program make the double click on the controller, a window will be opened click the 'Program file' option and select the hex file created for the project with Arduino IDE and click 'ok'. Fig. (**1.17**) shows how to Load the Hex file in the controller.

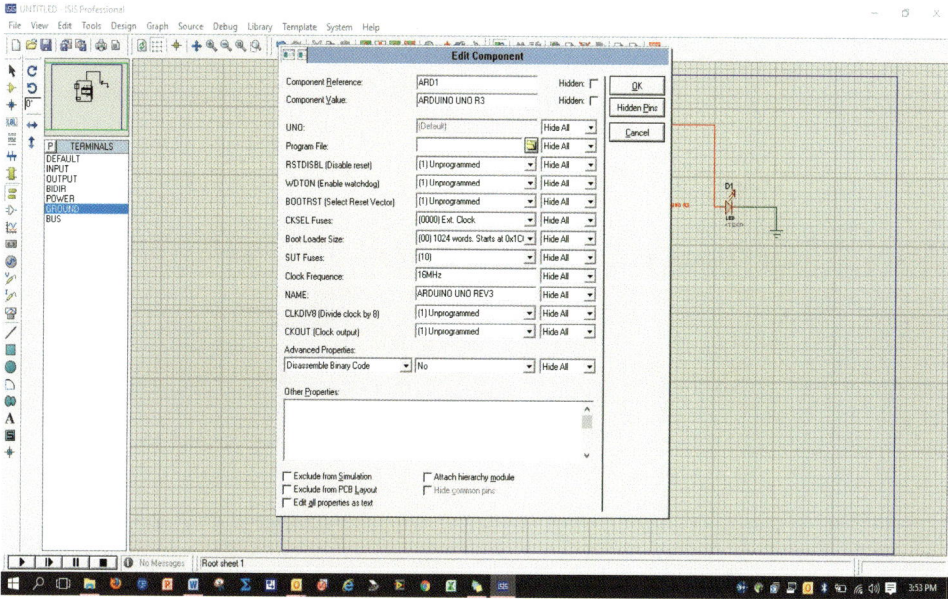

Fig. (1.17). Load the .Hex file in the controller.

Step 9- After loading the program in the controller, press play button on the left bottom side of the simulation model and observe the circuit behaviour. The simulation is complete.

CHAPTER 2

Arduino Interfacing with Display Devices

Abstract: Display devices are important part of any prototype developed by the learners. It is required to display the sensory values and other important information and check its validity at transmitter and receiver end. This chapter explores the interfacing of display devices with Arduino with the help of circuit diagrams and programs.

Keywords: Arduino, LED, Liquid Crystal Display, Seven Segment Display.

2.1. LIGHT EMITTING DIODE (LED)

Light emitting diode is most basic display device, which is mostly used to indicate the status of the system. For this purpose any color of LED can be used as per designer's choice. Fig. (**2.1**) shows the block diagram of LED interfacing with Arduino, comprises of Arduino board, power supply, resistors and LED.

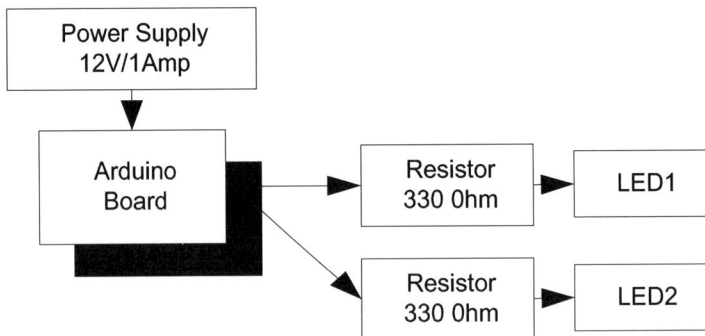

Fig. (2.1). Block diagram for LED interfacing with Arduino.

2.1.1. Circuit Diagram

Connect all the components to Arduino as per the connections as described-

1. LED1 indicator connected to pin13 of Arduino Uno through 330 ohm of resistor.
2. LED2 indicator connected to pin12 of Arduino Uno through 330 ohm of resistor.

Rajesh Singh, Anita Gehlot, Bhupendra Singh & Sushabhan Choudhury
All rights reserved-© 2018 Bentham Science Publishers

3. DC jack of +12 V power supply is connected to power supply DC jack of Arduino. Fig. (**2.2**) shows the circuit diagram of the system.

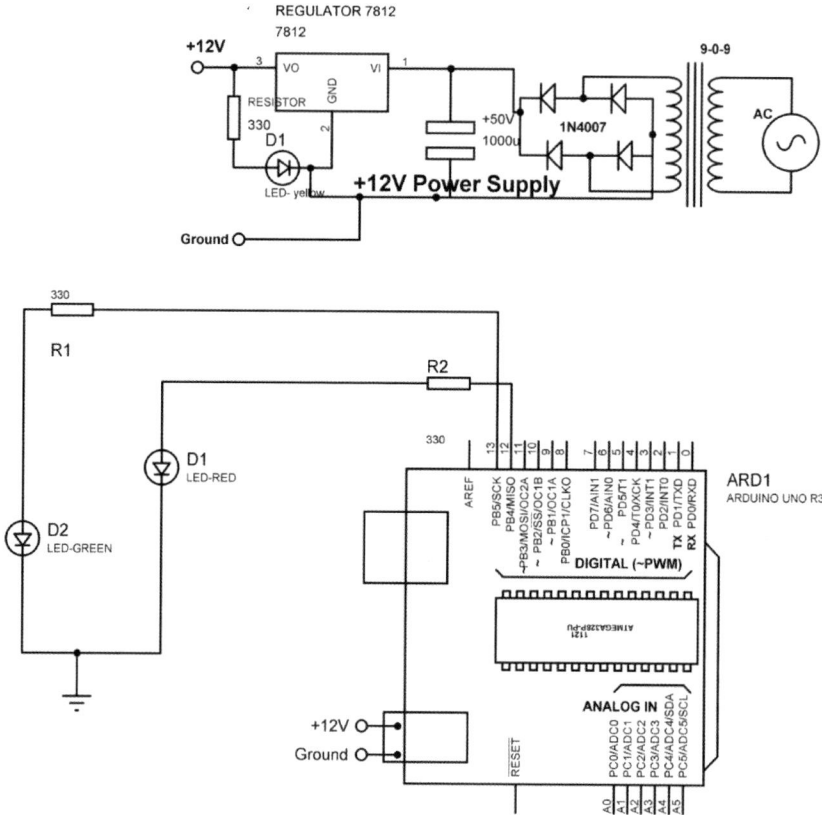

Fig. (2.2). Circuit diagram to interface LED with Arduino.

2.1.2. Program

Case1: (LED1 'ON')

int led_FIRST = 13;

int led_SECOND = 12;

void setup()

{

// initialize the digital pin as an output.

pinMode(led_FIRST, OUTPUT);

```
pinMode(led_SECOND, OUTPUT);

}

void loop()

{

digitalWrite(led_FIRST, HIGH); // turn the LED on by making the voltage HIGH

digitalWrite(led_SECOND, HIGH);

delay(1000); // wait for 1000 millisecond

digitalWrite(led_FIRST, LOW); // turn the LED off by making the voltage LOW

digitalWrite(led_SECOND, LOW);

delay(1000); // wait for 1000 millisecond

}

Case2: (LED2 'ON')

int led_FIRST = 13;

int led_SECOND = 12;

void setup()

{

// initialize the digital pin as an output.

pinMode(led_FIRST, OUTPUT);

pinMode(led_SECOND, OUTPUT);

}

void loop()

{

digitalWrite(led_FIRST, HIGH); // turn the LED ON/OFF by making the voltage
HIGH and LOW
```

digitalWrite(led_SECOND,LOW);

delay(1000); // wait for 1000 millisecond

digitalWrite(led_FIRST, LOW); // turn the LED ON/OFF by making the voltage HIGH and LOW

digitalWrite(led_SECOND, HIGH);

delay(1000); // wait for 1000 millisecond

digitalWrite(led_FIRST, HIGH); // turn the LED ON by making the pin voltage HIGH

digitalWrite(led_SECOND, HIGH);

delay(1000); // wait for 1000 millisecond

digitalWrite(led_FIRST, LOW); // turn the LED OFF by making the pin voltage LOW

digitalWrite(led_SECOND, LOW);

delay(1000); // wait for 1000 millisecond

}

2.1.3. Proteus Simulation Model

Connect the components with Arduino as described in section 2.1.1 in the virtual environment of Proteus simulator. Power supply need not to be connected in the virtual environment of Proteus. Load the program as described in section 2.1.2 and check the feasibility and working of the circuit. Fig. (**2.3**) shows the circuit simulation for the system.

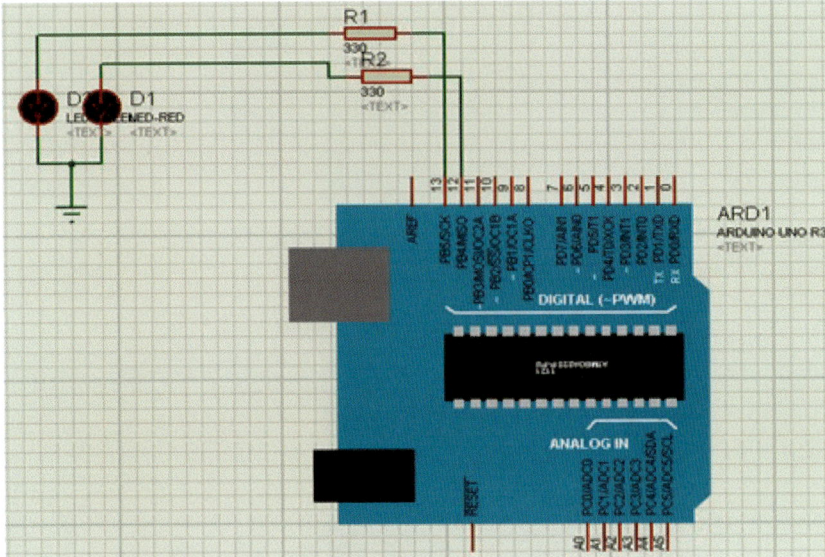

Fig. (2.3). Proteus simulation model for the Arduino interfacing with LED.

2.2. SEVEN SEGMENT DISPLAY

Seven segment is display unit which can display numeric values (0-9) and alphabets (A-F). It has seven LEDs connected in form of '8' terms as (a, b, c, d, e, f, g). It is of two types common cathode and common anode. In common cathode seven segment display cathode terminals of all the LEDs are connected to ground and anode terminals are connected to digital pins of the controller. In common anode seven segment display anode terminals of all the LEDs are connected to power supply and cathode terminals are connected to digital pins of the controller. Fig. (2.4) shows the block diagram of the system, comprises of Arduino board, power supply and seven segment display.

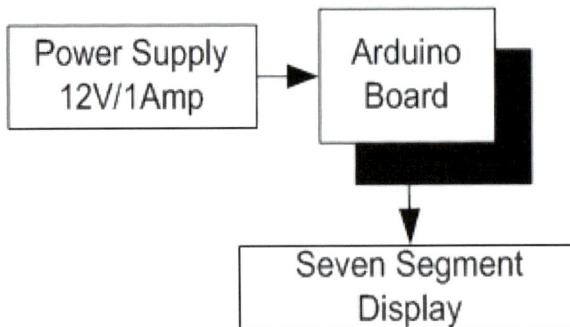

Fig. (2.4). Block diagram to interface seven segment display with Arduino.

2.2.1. Circuit Diagram

Circuit is explained for common cathode seven segment display unit. Connect all the components to Arduino as per the connections as described-

1. 'a' segment of seven segment connected to pin13 of Arduino Uno .
2. 'b' segment of seven segment connected to pin12 of Arduino Uno .
3. 'c' segment of seven segment at connected to pin11 of Arduino Uno .
4. 'd' segment of seven segment at connected to pin10 of Arduino Uno .
5. 'e' segment of seven segment at connected to pin9 of Arduino Uno .
6. 'f' segment of seven segment at connected to pin8 of Arduino Uno .
7. 'g' segment of seven segment at connected to pin7 of Arduino Uno .
8. DC jack of +12 V power supply is connected to power supply DC jack of Arduino.

Fig. (**2.5**) shows the circuit diagram of the system.

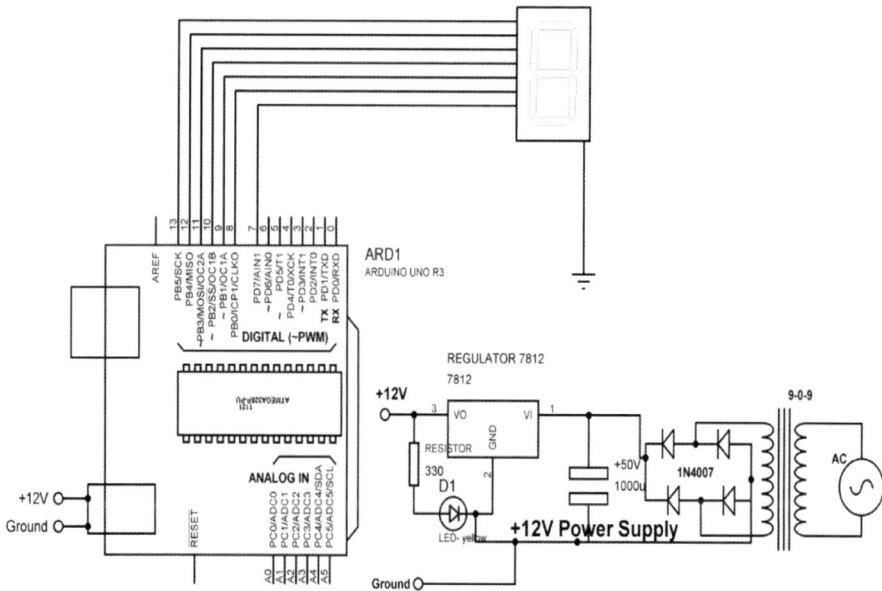

Fig. (2.5). Circuit Diagram to interface seven segment display with Arduino.

2.2.2. Program

int a = 13;

int b = 12;

```
int c = 11;

int d = 10;

int e = 9;

int f = 8;

int g = 7;

void setup()

{

pinMode(a, OUTPUT);

pinMode(b, OUTPUT);

pinMode(c, OUTPUT);

pinMode(d, OUTPUT);

pinMode(e, OUTPUT);

pinMode(f, OUTPUT);

pinMode(g, OUTPUT);


}

void loop()

{

digitalWrite(a, HIGH); // turn the 7 SEG ON as display ZERO

digitalWrite(b, HIGH);

digitalWrite(c, HIGH);

digitalWrite(d, HIGH);

digitalWrite(e, HIGH);

digitalWrite(f, HIGH);
```

digitalWrite(g, LOW);

delay(1000); // wait for a second

digitalWrite(a, LOW); // turn the 7 SEG ON as display ONE

digitalWrite(b, HIGH);

digitalWrite(c, HIGH);

digitalWrite(d, LOW);

digitalWrite(e, LOW);

digitalWrite(f, LOW);

digitalWrite(g, LOW);

delay(1000); // wait for a second

}

2.2.3. Proteus Simulation Model

Connect the components with Arduino as described in section 2.2.2 in the virtual environment of Proteus simulator. Power supply need not to be connected in the virtual environment of Proteus. Load the program as described in section 2.2.3 and check the feasibility and working of the circuit. Fig. (**2.6**) shows Proteus simulation model of the Arduino interfacing with Seven Segment

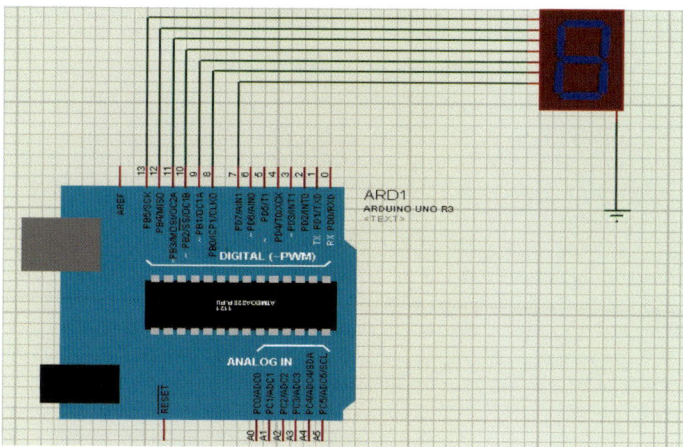

Fig. (2.6). Proteus simulation model for the Arduino interfacing with Seven Segment.

2.3. LIQUID CRYSTAL DISPLAY

Liquid crystal display unit is low cost display unit which can display alphanumeric values along with rows and columns. 16x2 LCD is mostly used in the projects. It means it has two rows and sixteen columns. Fig. (**2.7**) shows the block diagram of the system, comprises of Arduino, power supply and LCD.

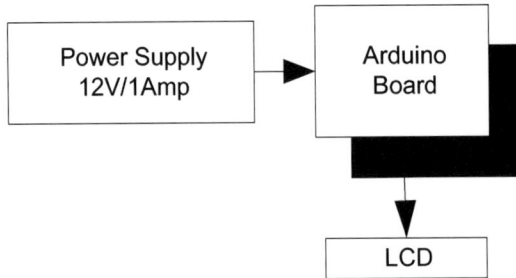

Fig. (2.7). Block diagram to interface LCD with Arduino.

2.3.1. Circuit Diagram

Connect all the components to Arduino as per the connections as described-

1. DC jack of +12 V power supply is connected to power supply DC jack of Arduino Uno
2. RS pin of LCD connected to pin12 of Arduino Uno
3. RW pin of LCD connected to GND pin of Arduino Uno
4. RS pin of LCD connected to pin11 of Arduino Uno
5. D4 pin of LCD connected to pin10 of Arduino Uno
6. D5 pin of LCD connected to pin9 of Arduino Uno
7. D6 pin of LCD connected to pin8 of Arduino Uno
8. D7 pin of LCD connected to pin7 of Arduino Uno
9. Pins1and 16 of LCD connected to GND pin of power supply patch.
10. Pins2 and 15 connected to +5V pin of power supply patch.

Fig. (**2.8**) shows circuit diagram to interface LCD with Arduino.

2.3.2. Program

```
#include <LiquidCrystal.h>

LiquidCrystal lcd(12, 11, 10, 9, 8, 7);

void setup()

{
```

```
lcd.begin(16, 2);

}

void loop()

{

lcd.clear();

lcd.setCursor(0, 0); // set the cursor to column 0, row 0

lcd.print("WELCOME");// print string on LCD


lcd.setCursor(0, 1);// set the cursor to column 0, row 0

lcd.print("UPES,DEHRADUN");// print string on LCD

}
```

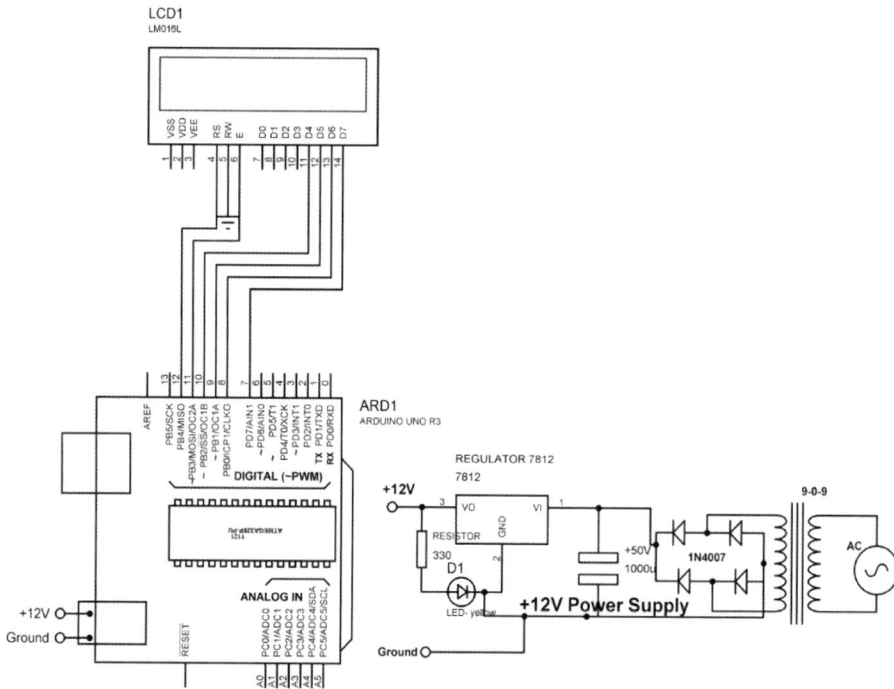

Fig. (2.8). Circuit Diagram to interface LCD with Arduino.

2.3.3. Proteus Simulation Model

Connect the components with Arduino as described in section 2.3.2 in the virtual environment of Proteus simulator. Power supply need not to be connected in the virtual environment of Proteus. Load the program as described in section 2.3.3 and check the feasibility and working of the circuit. Fig. (**2.9**) shows Proteus simulation model for the Arduino interfacing with LCD

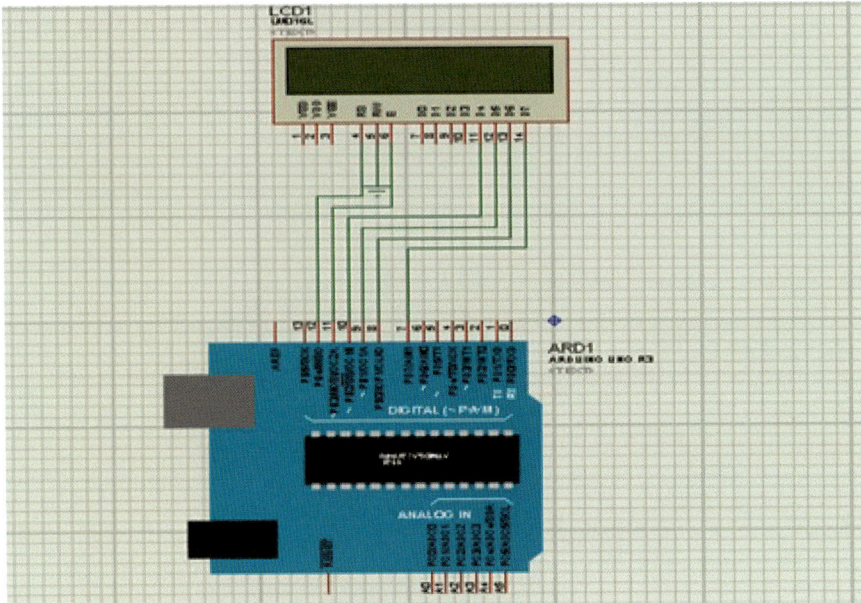

Fig. (2.9). Proteus simulation model for the Arduino interfacing with LCD.

CHAPTER 3

Arduino Interfacing with Digital Sensors

Abstract: Digital sensor gives digital output and changes the status with respect to change in conditions which can be processed through a controller unit. This chapter describes the interfacing of digital sensors like flame sensor, PIR sensor and Gas sensor with Arduino with the help of circuit diagram and programs.

Keywords: Arduino, Flame sensor, Gas sensor, PIR sensor.

3.1. FLAME SENSOR

Flame sensor or fire sensor acts as digital sensor which changes its output status with respect to the environmental changes. Fig. (**3.1**) shows the block diagram of the system, comprises of Arduino, power supply, flame sensor, LED. It is designed to sense the fire in the surrounding and corresponding change in the LED takes place.

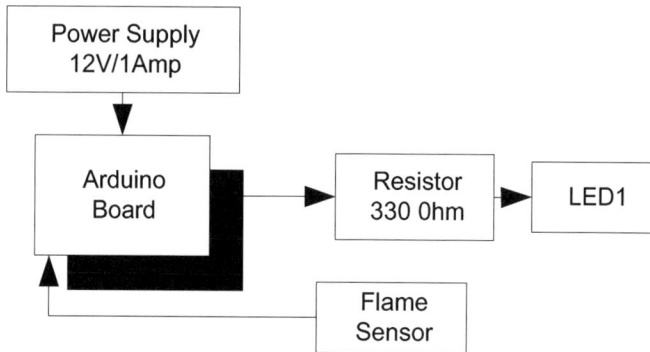

Fig. (3.1). Block diagram to interface flame sensor.

3.1.1. Circuit Diagram

Connect all the components to Arduino as per the connections as described-

1. Flame sensor 'OUT' pin is connected to pin3 of Arduino Uno.

Rajesh Singh, Anita Gehlot, Bhupendra Singh & Sushabhan Choudhury
All rights reserved-© 2018 Bentham Science Publishers

2. +Vcc and GND pins of flame sensor are connected to +5V and GND pin of power supply patch/explorer respectively.
3. Anode of LED1 is connected to pin2 of Arduino Uno through 330 ohm of resistor.
4. Cathode of LED1 is connected to 'GND'.
5. +12V power supply jack is connected to DC jack of Arduino Uno.

Fig. (**3.2**) shows circuit diagram to interface flame sensor.

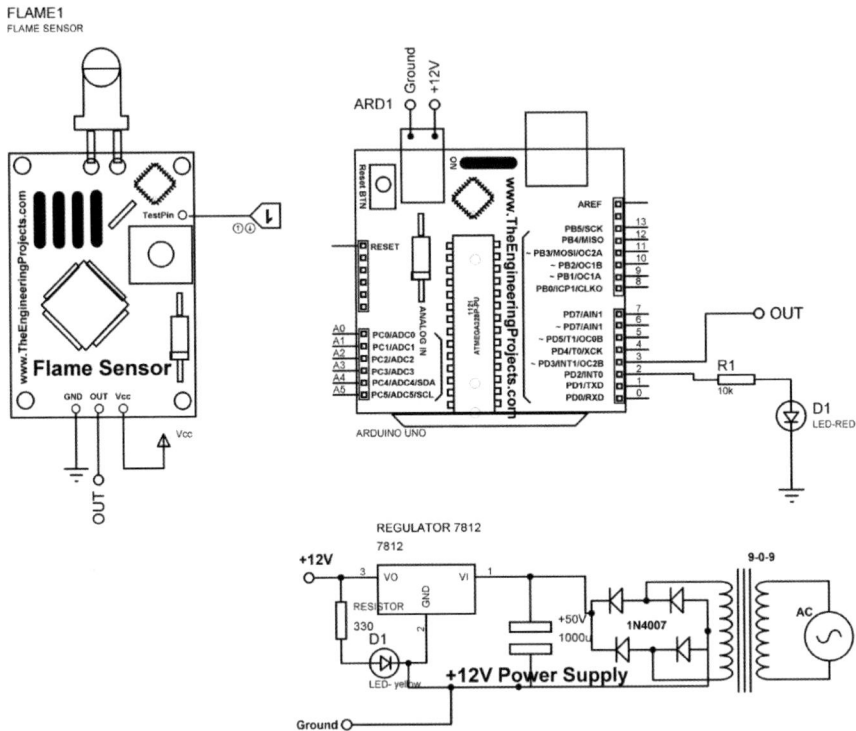

Fig. (3.2). Circuit diagram to interface flame sensor.

3.1.2. Program

int FlameOUT = 3;

int LED=2;

void setup()

{

```
pinMode(FlameOUT, INPUT_PULLUP);

pinMode(LED, OUTPUT);

}

void loop()

{

if(digitalRead(FlameOUT) == HIGH)

{

digitalWrite(LED,HIGH);

delay(20);

}

if(digitalRead(FlameOUT) == LOW)

{

digitalWrite(LED,LOW);

delay(20);

}

}
```

3.1.3. Proteus Simulation Model

Connect the components with Arduino as described in section 3.1.2 in the virtual environment of Proteus simulator. Power supply need not to be connected in the virtual environment of Proteus. As Proteus is virtual environment to make the change in the status of sensor a 'logic' is connected to logic state pin, which can be changed to '0' or '1' to check the working of sensor. Load the program as described in section 3.1.3 and check the feasibility and working of the circuit Fig. (**3.3**) shows the Proteus model for the system.

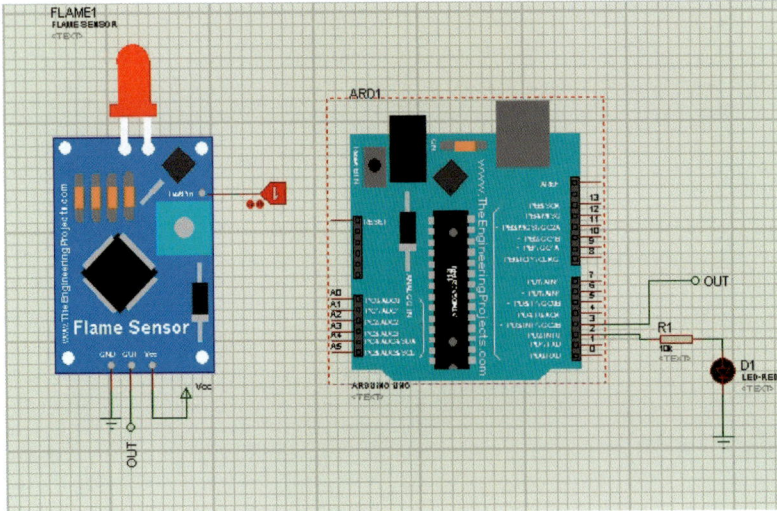

Fig. (3.3). Proteus simulation model of the Arduino interfacing with flame sensor.

3.2. PIR SENSOR

PIR sensor or motion sensor acts as digital sensor which changes its output status with respect to the motion of human. Fig. (**3.4**) shows the block diagram of the system, comprises of Arduino, power supply, PIR sensor, LED. It is designed to sense the human motion in the surrounding and corresponding change in the LED takes place.

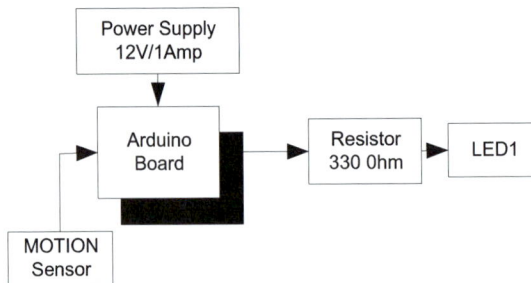

Fig. (3.4). Block diagram for the interfacing of PIR sensor.

3.2.1. Circuit Diagram

Connect all the components to Arduino as per the connections as described:

1. PIR sensor 'OUT pin' connected to pin3 of Arduino Uno.
2. +Vcc and GND pins of PIR sensor connected to +5Va n GND pins of power supply patch/explorer.

3. Anode of LED1 is connected to pin2 of Arduino Uno through 330 ohm of resistor.

4. Cathode of LED1 is connected to 'GND'.

5. +12V power supply jack is connected to DC jack of Arduino Uno.

Fig. (**3.5**) shows circuit diagram of the interfacing of PIR sensor.

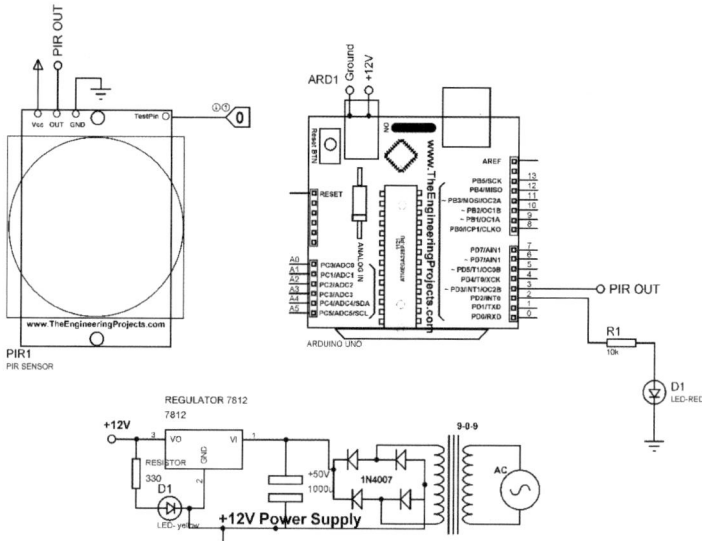

Fig. (3.5). Circuit diagram for the interfacing of PIR sensor.

3.2.3. Program

int calibrationTime = 30;

long unsigned int lowIn;

long unsigned int pause = 5000;

boolean lockLow = true;

boolean takeLowTime;

int PIRValue = 0;

int LED=2;

int PIRSENSOR=3;

```
void setup()
{
pinMode(PIRSENSOR, INPUT);
pinMode(LED,OUTPUT);
}
void loop()
{
if(digitalRead(PIRSENSOR) == HIGH)
{
if(lockLow)
{
PIRValue = 1;
lockLow = false;
digitalWrite(LED,HIGH);
delay(50);
}
takeLowTime = true;
}
if(digitalRead(PIRSENSOR) == LOW)
{
if(takeLowTime)
{
lowIn = millis();
takeLowTime = false;
```

```
}

if(!lockLow && millis() - lowIn > pause)

{

PIRValue = 0;

lockLow = true;

digitalWrite(LED,LOW);

delay(50);

}

} }
```

3.2.3. Proteus Simulation Model

Connect the components with Arduino as described in section 3.2.2 in the virtual environment of Proteus simulator. Power supply need not to be connected in the virtual environment of Proteus. As Proteus is virtual environment to make the change in the status of sensor a 'logic' is connected to logic state pin, which can be changed to '0' or '1' to check the working of sensor. Load the program as described in section 3.2.3 and check the feasibility and working of the circuit Fig. (**3.6**) shows the Proteus model for the system.

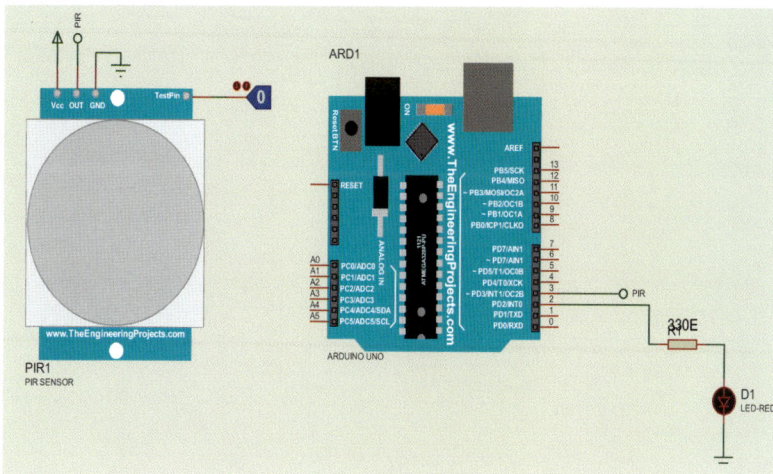

Fig. (3.6). Proteus simulation model of the Arduino interfacing with PIR sensor.

3.3. GAS SENSOR

Gas sensor can act as analog or digital output. Here gas sensor acts as digital sensor which changes its output status with respect to the environmental changes. Fig. (**3.7**) shows the block diagram of the system, comprises of Arduino, power supply, gas sensor, LED. It is designed to sense the fire in the surrounding and corresponding change in the LED takes place.

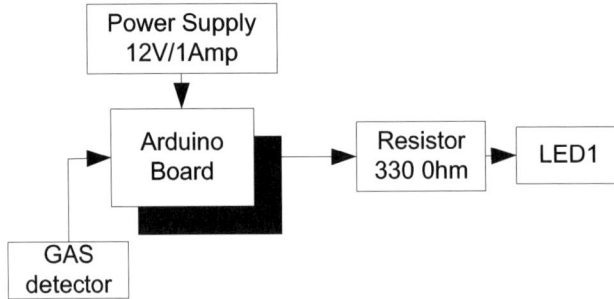

Fig. (**3.7**). Block diagram for the interfacing of Gas sensor.

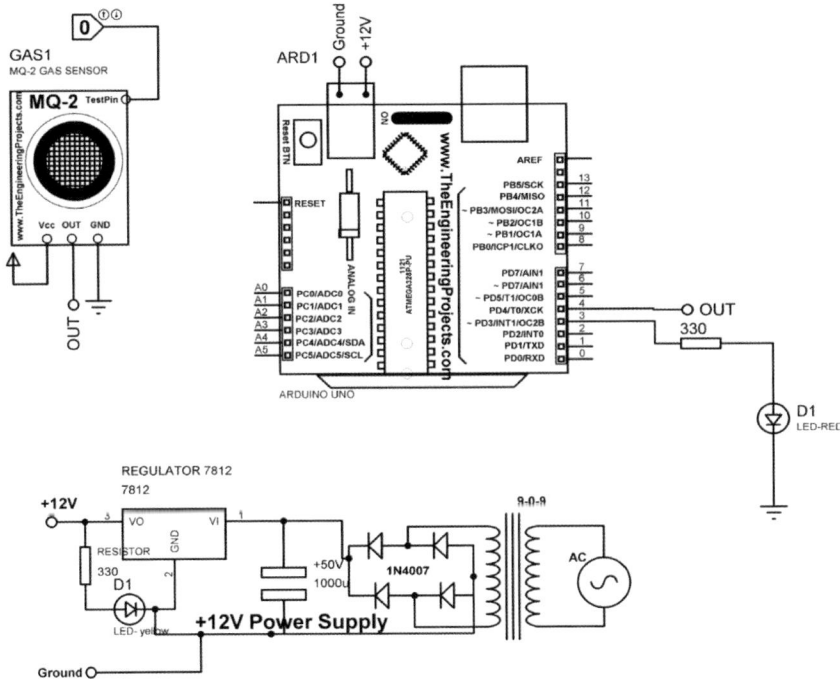

Fig. (**3.8**). Circuit diagram of the interfacing of Gas sensor.

3.3.1. Circuit Diagram

Connect all the components to Arduino as per the connections as described-

1. GAS sensor OUT pin connected to pin3 of Arduino Uno
2. +Vcc and GND pins of Gas sensor connected to +5Va n GND pins of power supply patch.
3. Anode of LED1 is connected to pin2 of Arduino Uno through 330 ohm of resistor.
4. Cathode of LED1 is connected to 'GND'.
5. +12V power supply jack is connected to DC jack of Arduino Uno.

Fig. (**3.8**) shows circuit diagram for the interfacing of Gas sensor.

3.3.2. Program

```
int GasSENSOR = 4;

int LED=3;

void setup()

{

pinMode(GasSENSOR, INPUT);

pinMode(LED,OUTPUT)

}

void loop()

{

if(digitalRead(GasSENSOR) == HIGH)

{

digitalWrite(LED,HIGH);

delay(50);

}

if(digitalRead(GasSENSOR) == LOW)
```

{

digitalWrite(LED,LOW);

delay(50);

}}

3.3.3. Proteus Simulation Model

Connect the components with Arduino as described in section 3.3.2 in the virtual environment of Proteus simulator. Power supply need not to be connected in the virtual environment of Proteus. As Proteus is virtual environment to make the change in the status of sensor a 'logic' is connected to logic state pin, which can be changed to '0' or '1' to check the working of sensor. Load the program as described in section 3.3.3 and check the feasibility and working of the circuit Fig. (**3.9**) shows the Proteus model for the system.

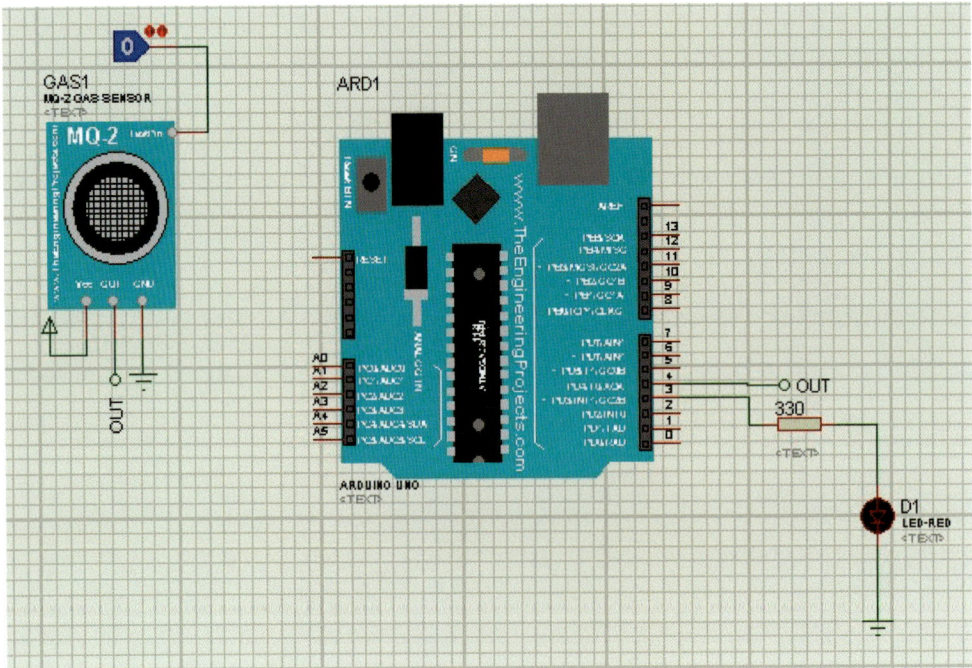

Fig. (3.9). Proteus simulation model of the Arduino interfacing with gas sensor.

CHAPTER 4

Arduino Interfacing with Analog Sensors

Abstract: Analog sensor gives analog output and changes the status with respect to change in conditions which can be processed through a controller unit. This chapter describes the interfacing of analog sensors like ultrasonic sensor and temperature sensor with Arduino with the help of circuit diagram and programs.

Keywords: Arduino, Analog sensor, Temperature sensor, Ultrasonic sensor.

4.1. ULTRASONIC SENSOR

Ultrasonic sensor is an analog sensor which changes its output status with respect to the change in the distance from an object. Fig. (**4.1**) shows the block diagram of the system, comprises of Arduino, power supply, ultrasonic sensor, LCD. It is designed to measure the distance from an object and corresponding change is displayed on LCD.

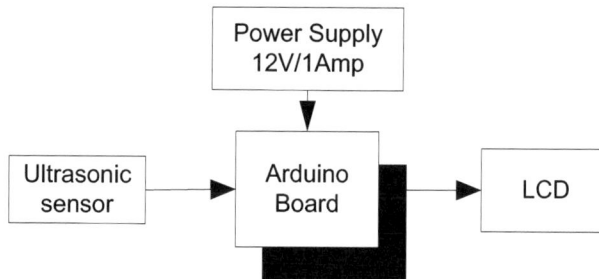

Fig. (4.1). Block diagram of the interfacing of ultrasonic sensor.

4.1.1. Circuit Diagram

Connect all the components to Arduino as per the connections as described-

1. Trigger pin is connected to pin3 of Arduino Uno.
2. Echo pin is connected to pin2 of Arduino Uno.
3. +Vcc and GND pins of ultrasonic sensor are connected to +5V and GND pins of power supply patch respectively.

Rajesh Singh, Anita Gehlot, Bhupendra Singh & Sushabhan Choudhury
All rights reserved-© 2018 Bentham Science Publishers

4. RS pin of LCD is connected to pin12 of Arduino Uno.
5. RW pin of LCD is connected to GND pin of Arduino Uno.
6. RS pin of LCD is connected to pin11 of Arduino Uno.
7. D4 pin of LCD is connected to pin10 of Arduino Uno.
8. D5 pin of LCD is connected to pin9 of Arduino Uno.
9. D6 pin of LCD is connected to pin8 of Arduino Uno.
10. D7 pin of LCD is connected to pin7 of Arduino Uno.
11. Pins 1and 16 are connected to GND pin of power supply patch.
12. Pins 2 and 15 are connected to +5V pin of power supply patch.
13. +12V power supply jack is connected to DC jack of Arduino Uno.

Note- To vary the intensity of LCD Potentiometer can be used. Variable terminal of 10K POT is connected to pin 3 of LCD. Two-fixed terminals are connected to +5V and GND pin of patch respectively. Vary the value to change the background light intensity.

Fig. (**4.2**) shows circuit diagram for the interfacing of ultrasonic sensor.

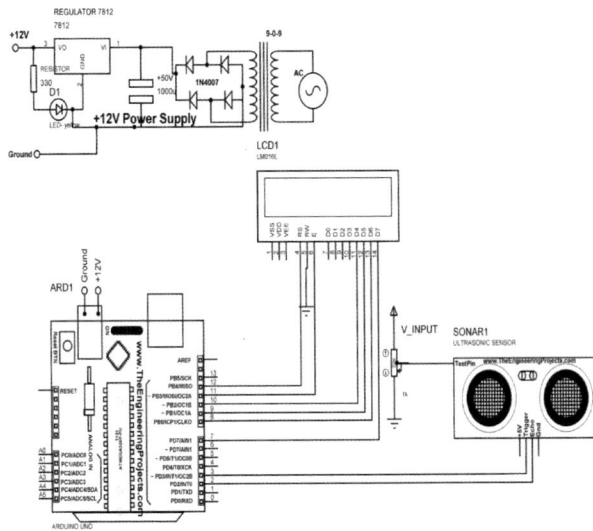

Fig. (4.2). Circuit diagram for the interfacing of ultrasonic sensor.

4.1.2. Program

#include <LiquidCrystal.h>

LiquidCrystal lcd(12, 11, 10, 9, 8, 7);

const int pingPin = 3; // Trigger Pin of Ultrasonic Sensor

```
const int echoPin = 2; // Echo Pin of Ultrasonic Sensor
void setup()
{
lcd.begin(16,2); // initialize the 16*2 LCD
}
void loop()
{
lcd.clear();
long duration, inches, cm;
pinMode(pingPin, OUTPUT);
digitalWrite(pingPin, LOW);
delayMicroseconds(2);
digitalWrite(pingPin, HIGH);
delayMicroseconds(10);
digitalWrite(pingPin, LOW);
pinMode(echoPin, INPUT);
duration = pulseIn(echoPin, HIGH);
inches = microsecondsToInches(duration);
cm = microsecondsToCentimeters(duration);
lcd.setCursor(0, 0);
lcd.print(inches);
lcd.print("inches");
lcd.setCursor(0, 1);
lcd.print(cm);
```

lcd.print("cm");

delay(100);

}

long microsecondsToInches(long microseconds)

{

return microseconds / 74 / 2;

}

long microsecondsToCentimeters(long microseconds)

{

return microseconds / 29 / 2;

}

4.1.3. Proteus Simulation Model

Connect the components with Arduino as described in section 4.1.2 in the virtual environment of Proteus simulator. Power supply need not to be connected in the virtual environment of Proteus. As Proteus is virtual environment to make the change in the status of sensor a potentiometer is connected to sensor, which is used to check the working of sensor. Load the program as described in section 4.1.2 and check the feasibility and working of the circuit. Fig. (**4.3**) shows the Proteus model for the system.

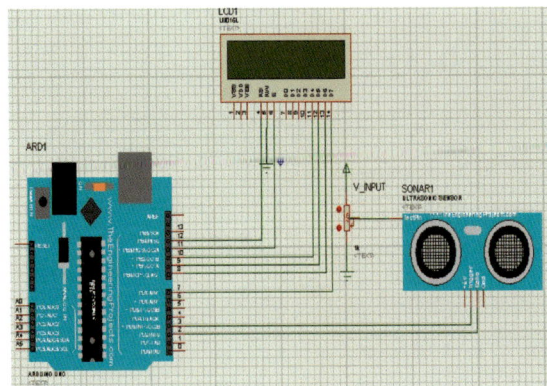

Fig. (4.3). Proteus simulation model for the Arduino interfacing with ultrasonic sensor.

4.2. TEMPERATURE (LM35) SENSOR

LM35 is a temperature sensor which changes its output status with respect to the change in the distance from an object. Fig. (**4.4**) shows the block diagram of the system, comprises of Arduino, power supply, LM35 sensor, load, LCD. It is designed to measure the temperature and switch on the load (fan, here bulb is connected to demonstrate). To make load 'ON' load is connected through a transistor and relay. LCD is connected to display the value of temperature.

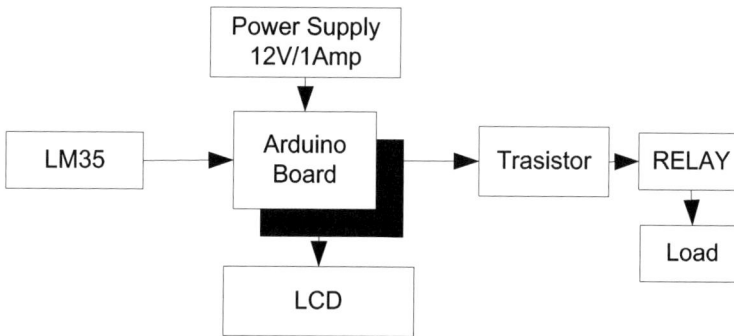

Fig. (4.4). Block diagram for the interfacing of temperature sensor.

4.2.1. Circuit Diagram

Connect all the components to Arduino as per the connections as described-

1. Analog OUT pin of temperature sensor is connected to A0 pin of Arduino Uno.
2. +Vcc and GND pins of sensor are connected to +5Va n GND pis of power supply patch/explorer respectively.
3. RS pin of LCD is connected to pin12 of Arduino Uno.
4. RW pin of LCD is connected to GND pin of Arduino Uno.
5. RS pin of LCD is connected to pin11 of Arduino Uno.
6. D4 pin of LCD is connected to pin 5 of Arduino Uno.
7. D5 pin of LCD is connected to pin4 of Arduino Uno.
8. D6 pin of LCD is connected to pin3 of Arduino Uno.
9. D7 pin of LCD is connected to pin2 of Arduino Uno.
10. Pins 1and 16 are connected to GND pin of power supply patch.
11. Pins 2 and 15 are connected to +5V pin of power supply patch.
12. +12V power supply jack is connected to DC jack of Arduino Uno.
13. Relay board input pin is connected to collector of transistor 2N2222.
14. Emitter of transistor is connected to 'GND'.
15. Base of transistor is connected to pin 9 of the Arduino Uno trough transistor.

16. One terminal of AC source 220V is connected to common terminal of relay.
17. Other terminal of AC source is connected to one terminal of load.
18. Other terminal of load is connected to 'NO' pin of relay.

Note- To vary the intensity of LCD Potentiometer can be used. Variable terminal of 10K POT is connected to pin 3 of LCD. Two-fixed terminals are connected to +5V and GND pin of patch respectively. Vary the value to change the background light intensity.

Fig. (**4.5**) shows circuit diagram for the interfacing of temperature sensor.

Fig. (4.5). Circuit diagram for the interfacing of temperature sensor.

4.2.2. Program

#include <LiquidCrystal.h>

LiquidCrystal lcd(12, 11, 5, 4, 3, 2);

void setup()

{

lcd.begin(16, 2);// initialize the LCD

pinMode(9, OUTPUT);

```
lcd.print("LM35 READING");

lcd.setCursor(0, 1);

lcd.print("System");

delay(1000);

lcd.clear();

}

void loop()

{

int sensorValue = analogRead(A0);

int TEMP=sensorValue/2;

lcd.setCursor(0, 0);

lcd.print("TEMP:");

lcd.print(TEMP);

delay(200);

if (TEMP >=50)

{

lcd.clear();

digitalWrite(9, HIGH);

lcd.setCursor(0, 1);

lcd.print("OVER TEMP");

delay(20);

}

else

{
```

lcd.clear();

digitalWrite(9, LOW);

lcd.setCursor(0, 1);

lcd.print("NORMAL TEMP ");

delay(20);

}

}

4.2.3. Proteus Simulation Model

Connect the components with Arduino as described in section 4.2.2 in the virtual environment of Proteus simulator. Power supply need not to be connected in the virtual environment of Proteus. As Proteus is virtual environment to make the change in the status of sensor a potentiometer is connected to sensor, which is used to check the working of sensor. Load the program as described in section 4.2.2 and check the feasibility and working of the circuit. Fig. (**4.6**) shows the Proteus model for the system.

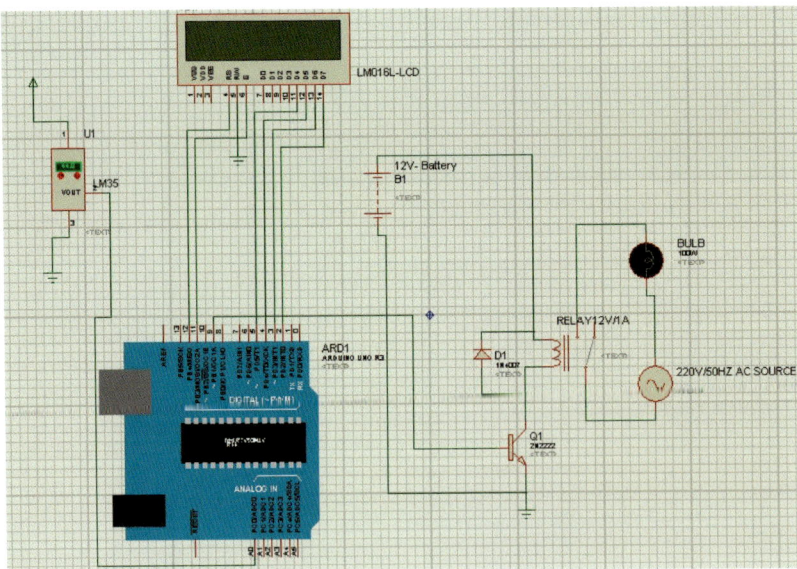

Fig. (4.6). Proteus simulation model for the Arduino interfacing with LM35 sensor.

CHAPTER 5

Arduino Interfacing with Actuators

Abstract: An actuator is a component which is responsible for moving or controlling a mechanism. An actuator requires a control signal and a source of energy. This chapter explains the working of actuator with the help of different methods.

Keywords: AC motor, Arduino, DC motor, L293D, Stepper motor, Servo motor.

5.1. DC MOTOR CONTROL WITH TRANSISTOR 'H' BRIDGE

A DC motor is a device that converts electrical energy into mechanical energy. It has vital importance for the industry. Fig. (**5.1**) shows the block diagram of the system, comprises of Arduino, power supply, DC motor, LED. It is designed to control the DC motor with 'H' bridge (2N2222), LEDs are connected to check the change in the status of inputs to motor in order to make it move in forward and reverse direction. To make H bridge four 2N2222 transistors are used- Q1, Q2, Q3, Q4.

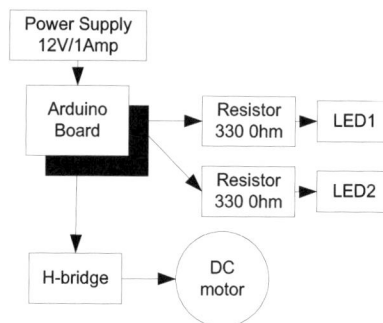

Fig. (**5.1**). Block diagram for the interfacing of DC motor.

5.1.1. Circuit Diagram

Connect all the components to Arduino as per the connections as described-

1. Make collector of Q1 & Q2 common and connect to positive terminal of +12V DC.
2. Make emitter of Q3 & Q4 common and connect to negative terminal of +12V DC and 'GND'.

Rajesh Singh, Anita Gehlot, Bhupendra Singh & Sushabhan Choudhury
All rights reserved-© 2018 Bentham Science Publishers

3. Make base of Q1 & Q4 common and connect to pin9 of Arduino.
4. Make base of Q2 & Q3 common and connect to pin10 of Arduino.
5. LEDs are also connected parallel to inputs of H -bridge.
6. +12V DC jack of power supply is connected to DC jack of Arduino Uno.

Fig. (**5.2**) shows circuit diagram for the interfacing of DC motor.

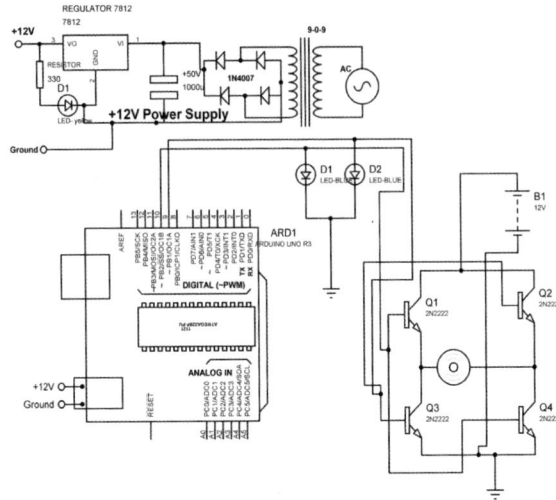

Fig. (5.2). Circuit diagram for the interfacing of DC motor.

5.1.2. Program

```
int MPIN1 = 10;

int MPIN2 = 9;

void setup()

{

// initialize pin10 and 9 as output

pinMode(MPIN1, OUTPUT);

pinMode(MPIN2, OUTPUT);

}

void loop()

{
```

digitalWrite(MPIN1, HIGH); // make 10 and 9 pin HIGH and LOW respectively

digitalWrite(MPIN2, LOW);

delay(1000); // wait for a 1000 millisecond

digitalWrite(MPIN1, LOW); // make 9 and 10 pin HIGH and LOW respectively

digitalWrite(MPIN2, HIGH);

delay(1000); // wait for a 1000 millisecond

}

5.1.3. Proteus Simulation Model

Connect the components with Arduino as described in section 5.1.1 in the virtual environment of Proteus simulator. Power supply need not to be connected in the virtual environment of Proteus. Load the program as described in section 5.1.2 and check the feasibility and working of the circuit. Fig. (**5.3**) shows the Proteus model for the system.

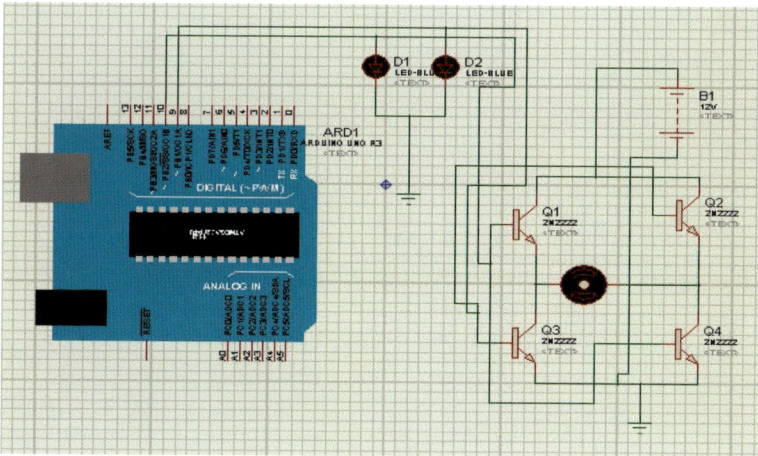

Fig. (5.3). Proteus simulation model for the Arduino interfacing with DC motor.

5.2. DC MOTOR CONTROL WITH L293D

L293D is 14 pin motor driver IC. DC motor upto 12V/1A ca be controlled with this.Fig. (**5.4**) shows the block diagram of the system, comprises of Arduino, power supply, DC motor, L293D, LED. It is designed to control the DC motor with IC L293D. LEDs are connected to check the change in the status of inputs to motor in order to make it move in forward and reverse direction.

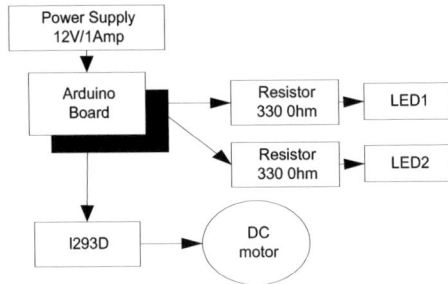

Fig. (5.4). Block diagram to control DC motor with L293D.

5.2.1. Circuit Diagram

Connect all the components to Arduino as per the connections as described-

1. Input pins 2 and 7 of L293D IC are connected to 10 and 9 pins of Arduino Uno.
2. Output pins 3 and 8 of L293D IC are connected to +ve and –ve terminals of DC motor respectively.
3. +12V DC jack of power supply is connected to DC jack of Arduino Uno.
4. Pins 1,9 and 16 of L293D are connected to +5V.
5. Pins 4,5 and 12, 13 of L293D are connected to GND.
6. Pin 8 of L293D is connected to +12V power supply.
7. LEDs are connected parallel to input pins 2 & 7 of L293D.

Fig. (**5.5**) shows circuit diagram to control DC motor with L293D.

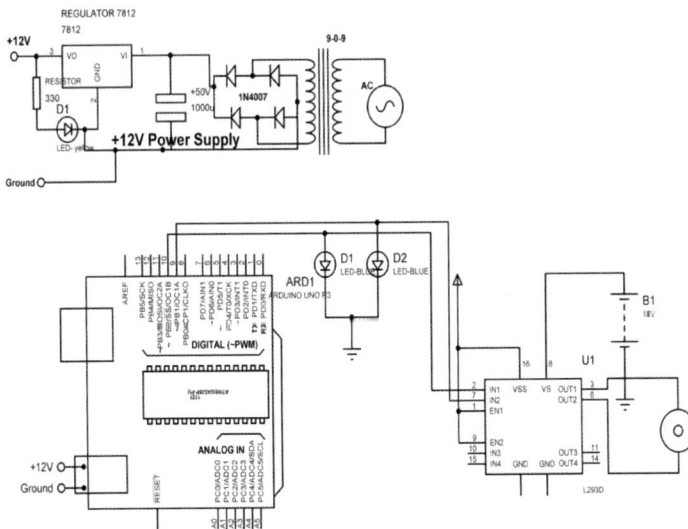

Fig. (5.5). Circuit diagram to control DC motor with L293D.

5.2.2. Program

```
int MPIN1 = 10;

int MPIN2 = 9;

void setup()

{

// initialize the digital pin as an output.

pinMode(MPIN1, OUTPUT);

pinMode(MPIN2, OUTPUT);

}

void loop()

{

clockwise();

delay(2000); // wait for a 1000 millisecond

anticlockwise();

delay(2000); // wait for a 1000 millisecond

}

clockwise()

{

digitalWrite(MPIN1, HIGH); // make pin 10 as HIGH and 9 as LOW

digitalWrite(MPIN2, LOW);

}

anticlockwise()

{

digitalWrite(MPIN1, LOW); // make pin 10 as LOW and 9 as HIGH
```

digitalWrite(MPIN2, HIGH);

}

5.2.3. Proteus Simulation Model

Connect the components with Arduino as described in section 5.2.1 in the virtual environment of Proteus simulator. Power supply need not to be connected in the virtual environment of Proteus. Load the program as described in section 5.2.2 and check the feasibility and working of the circuit. Fig. (**5.3**) shows the Proteus model for the system.

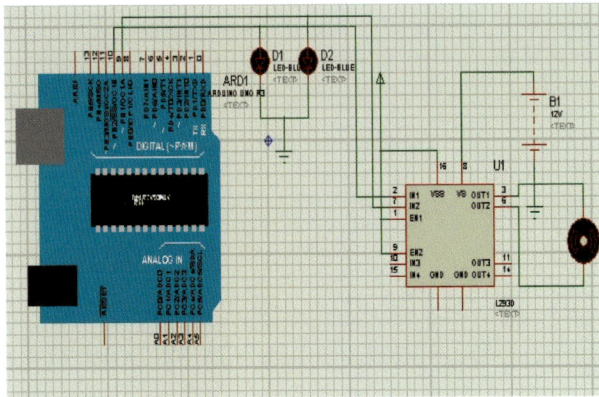

Fig. (5.6). Proteus simulation model for the Arduino interfacing with DC motor.

5.3. STEPPER MOTOR

Stepper motor can be controlled to move in the steps with the help of L293D. Fig. (**5.7**) shows the block diagram of the system, comprises of Arduino, power supply, stepper motor, L293D, LEDs. It is designed to control the stepper motor with IC L293D. LEDs are connected to check the change in the status of inputs to motor in order to make it move in forward and reverse direction.

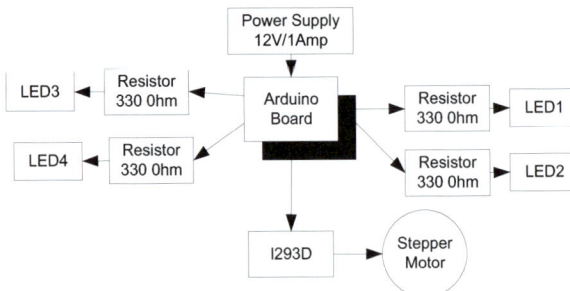

Fig. (5.7). Block diagram for the interfacing of stepper motor with Arduino.

5.3.1. Circuit Diagram

Connect all the components to Arduino as per the connections as described-

1. Input pins 2, 7, 10 and 15 of L293D IC are connected to 7, 6, 5 and 4 pins of Arduino Uno.
2. Output pins 3,6,11 and 14 of L293D IC are connected to A,B,C and D phase terminals stepper motor.
3. LEDs are also connected parallel to inputs of L293D.
4. +12V DC jack of power supply is connected to DC jack of Arduino Uno.
5. Pins 1,9 and 16 of L293D are connected to +5V.
6. Pins 4,5 and 12, 13 are connected to GND.
7. Pin 8 of L293D is connected to +12 pin of power supply.

Fig. (**5.8**) Shows circuit diagram for the interfacing of stepper motor with Arduino.

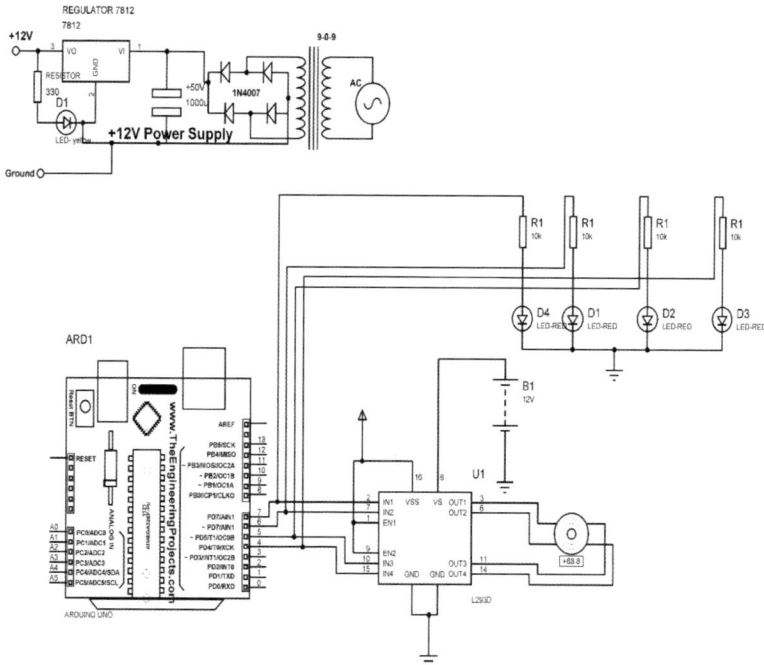

Fig. (5.8). Circuit diagram for the interfacing of stepper motor with Arduino.

5.3.2. Program

int MPIN1 = 7;

int MPIN2 = 6;

```
int MPIN3 = 5;

int MPIN4 = 4;

void setup()

{

// initialize the digital pin as an output.

pinMode(MPIN1, OUTPUT);

pinMode(MPIN2, OUTPUT);

pinMode(MPIN3, OUTPUT);

pinMode(MPIN4, OUTPUT);

}

void loop()

{

digitalWrite(MPIN1, LOW);

digitalWrite(MPIN2, LOW);

digitalWrite(MPIN3, LOW);

digitalWrite(MPIN4, HIGH);

delay(20); // wait for a 20 millisecond

digitalWrite(MPIN1, LOW);

digitalWrite(MPIN2, LOW);

digitalWrite(MPIN3, HIGH);

digitalWrite(MPIN4, LOW);

delay(20); // wait for a 20 millisecond

digitalWrite(MPIN1, LOW);

digitalWrite(MPIN2, HIGH);
```

```
digitalWrite(MPIN3, LOW);

digitalWrite(MPIN4, LOW);

delay(20); // wait for a 20 millisecond

digitalWrite(MPIN1, HIGH);

digitalWrite(MPIN2, LOW);

digitalWrite(MPIN3, LOW);

digitalWrite(MPIN4, LOW);

delay(20); // wait for a 20 millisecond

}
```

5.3.3. Proteus Simulation Model

Connect the components with Arduino as described in section 5.3.1 in the virtual environment of Proteus simulator. Power supply need not to be connected in the virtual environment of Proteus. Load the program as described in section 5.3.2 and check the feasibility and working of the circuit. Fig. (**5.9**) shows the Proteus model for the system.

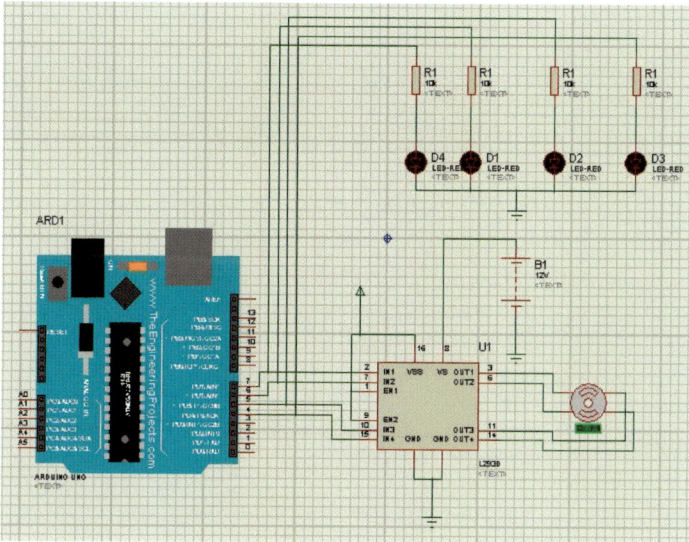

Fig. (5.9). Proteus simulation model for the Arduino interfacing with stepper motor.

5.4. SERVO MOTOR

Servo motor can be controlled with the help of PWM pin of Arduino. Fig. (**5.10**) shows the block diagram of the system, comprises of Arduino, power supply, servo motor, LCD. LCD is connected to display the change in the status of motor.

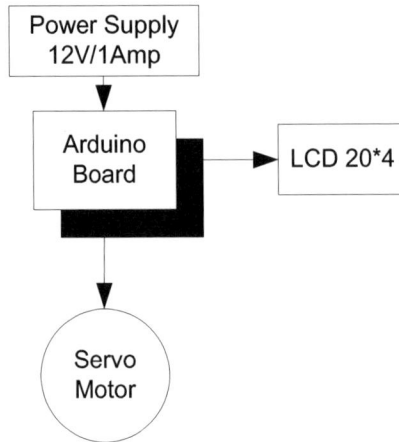

Fig. (5.10). Block diagram for the interfacing of servo motor with Arduino.

5.4.1. Circuit Diagram

Connect all the components to Arduino as per the connections as described-

1. RS pin of LCD is connected to pin12 of Arduino Uno.
2. RW pin of LCD is connected to GND pin of Arduino Uno.
3. RS pin of LCD is connected to pin11 of Arduino Uno.
4. D4 pin of LCD is connected to pin10 of Arduino Uno.
5. D5 pin of LCD is connected to pin9 of Arduino Uno.
6. D6 pin of LCD is connected to pin8 of Arduino Uno.
7. D7 pin of LCD is connected to pin7 of Arduino Uno.
8. Pins 1and 16 are connected to GND pin of power supply patch.
9. Pins 2 and 15 are connected to +5V pin of power supply patch.
10. +12V power supply jack is connected to DC jack of Arduino Uno.
11. Servo PWM pin is connected to pin3 of Arduino Uno.
12. +Vcc and GND pins of servo motor are connected to +5V and GND respectively.

Fig. (**5.11**) shows circuit diagram for the interfacing of servo motor with Arduino.

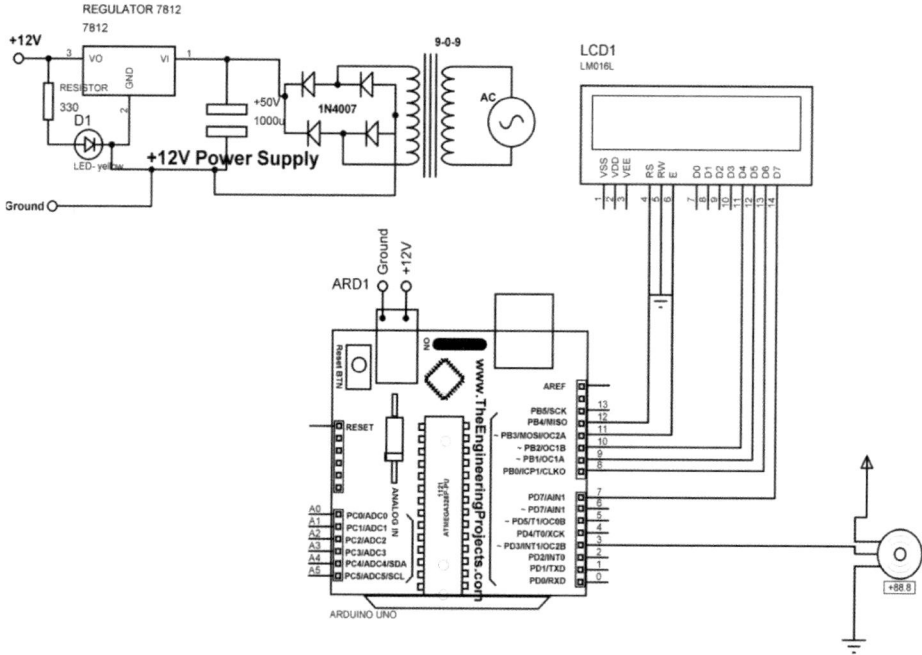

Fig. (5.11). Circuit diagram for the interfacing of servo motor with Arduino.

5.4.2. Program

#include <LiquidCrystal.h>

#include <Servo.h>

// initialize the library of LCD RS,E,D4,D5,D6,D7

LiquidCrystal lcd(12, 11, 10, 9, 8, 7);

Servo myservo; // create servo object to control a servo

// a maximum of eight servo objects can be created

int pos = 0; // variable to store the servo position

void setup()

{

lcd.begin(16, 2);// initialize the LCD

myservo.attach(3); // connect servo at pin3

```
}

void loop()

{

for(pos = 0; pos < 180; pos += 1) // goes from 0 degrees to 180 degrees(step of one degree)

{

lcd.clear();

myservo.write(pos); // tell servo to go to position in variable 'pos'

lcd.print(pos);// display position on LCD

delay(15); // delay 15ms

}

for(pos = 180; pos>=1; pos-=1) // goes from 180 degrees to 0 degrees

{

lcd.clear();

myservo.write(pos); // tell servo to go to position in variable 'pos'

lcd.print(pos);// display position on LCD

delay(15); // delay 15ms

}

}
```

5.4.3. Proteus Simulation Model

Connect the components with Arduino as described in section 5.4.1 in the virtual environment of Proteus simulator. Power supply need not to be connected in the virtual environment of Proteus. Load the program as described in section 5.3.2 and check the feasibility and working of the circuit. Fig. (**5.12**) shows the Proteus model for the system.

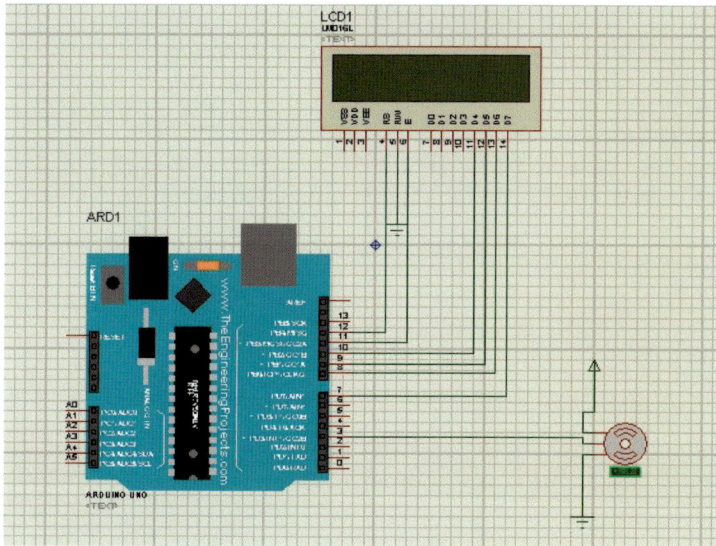

Fig. (5.12). Proteus simulation model of the Arduino interfacing with servo motor.

5.5. SERVO MOTOR CONTROL WITH POT

Servo motor can be controlled with the help of knob(POT). Fig. (**5.13**) shows the block diagram of the system, comprises of Arduino, power supply, servo motor, LCD, POT. LCD is connected to display the change in the status of motor.

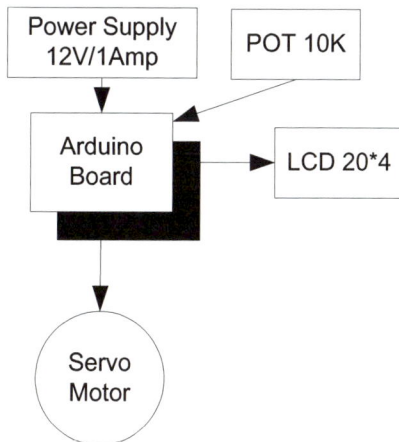

Fig. (5.13). Block diagram to control servo motor with POT.

5.5.1. Circuit Diagram

Connect all the components to Arduino as per the connections as described-

1. RS pin of LCD is connected to pin12 of Arduino Uno.
2. RW pin of LCD is connected to GND pin of Arduino Uno.
3. RS pin of LCD is connected to pin11 of Arduino Uno.
4. D4 pin of LCD is connected to pin10 of Arduino Uno.
5. D5 pin of LCD is connected to pin9 of Arduino Uno.
6. D6 pin of LCD is connected to pin8 of Arduino Uno.
7. D7 pin of LCD is connected to pin7 of Arduino Uno.
8. Pins 1and 16 of LCD are connected to GND pin of power supply patch.
9. Pins 2 and 15 of LCD are connected to +5V pin of power supply patch.
10. +12V power supply jack is connected to DC jack of Arduino Uno.
11. Servo PWM pin is connected to pin3 of Arduino Uno.
12. +Vcc and GND pins of servo motor are connected to +5V and GND.
13. 10K POT variable terminal is connected to analog pin A0.
14. Fixed terminal of 10K POT is connected to +5V and GND of power supply.

Fig. (**5.14**) shows circuit diagram to control servo motor with POT.

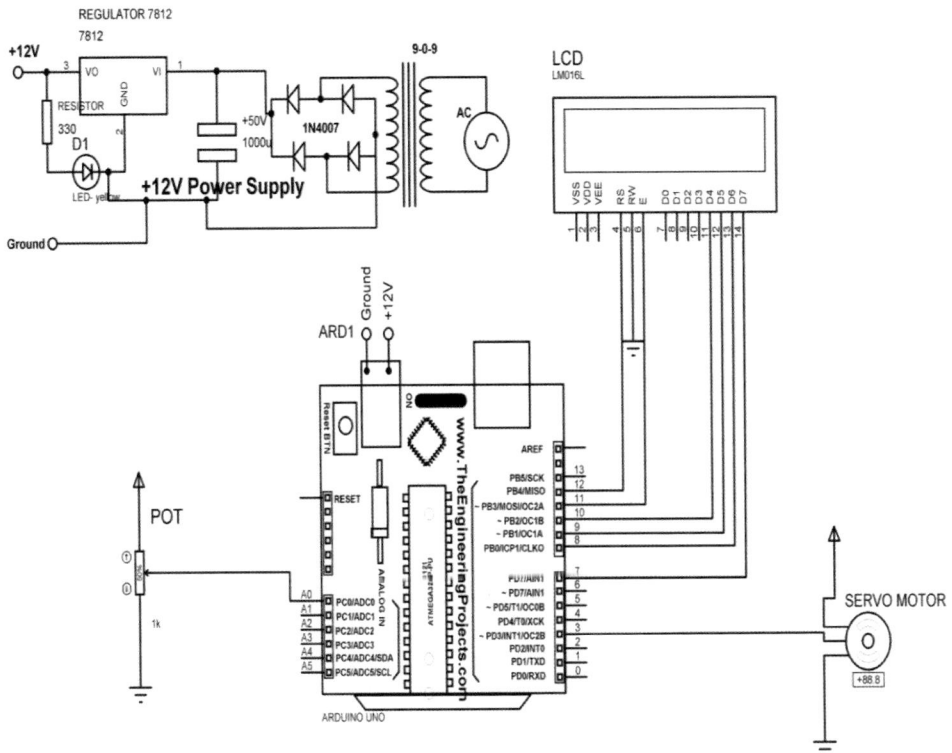

Fig. (5.14). Circuit diagram to control servo motor with POT.

5.5.2. Program

```
#include <LiquidCrystal.h>

#include <Servo.h>

// initialize the library of LCD (RS,E,D4,D5,D6,D7)

LiquidCrystal lcd(12, 11, 10, 9, 8, 7);

Servo myservo; // create servo object to control a servo

int pos = 0; // variable to store the servo position

void setup()

{

myservo.attach(3); // attaches the servo on pin 9 to the servo object

}

void loop()

{

int val = analogRead(A0); // READ analog pin A0

val = map(val, 0, 1023, 0, 179); // scale the angle

myservo.write(val); // sets the servo position according to the scaled value

lcd.print(val); // display position on LCD

delay(15); // waits for the servo to get there

}
```

5.5.3. Proteus Simulation Model

Connect the components with Arduino as described in section 5.5.1 in the virtual environment of Proteus simulator. Power supply need not to be connected in the virtual environment of Proteus. Load the program as described in section 5.5.2 and check the feasibility and working of the circuit. Fig. (**5.15**) shows the Proteus model for the system.

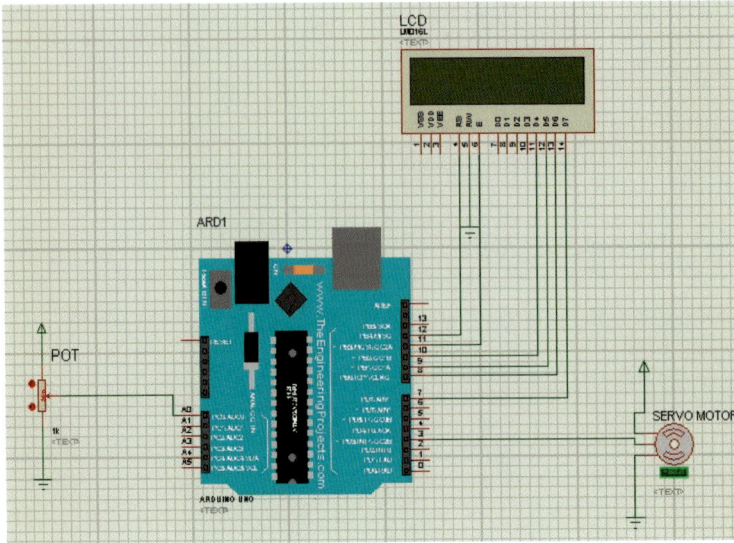

Fig. (5.15). Proteus simulation model of the Arduino interfacing with servo motor.

5.6. AC MOTOR

AC motor can be controlled with the help of relay. Fig. (**5.16**) shows the block diagram of the system, comprises of Arduino, power supply, AC motor, relay. LCD is connected to display the change in the status of motor.

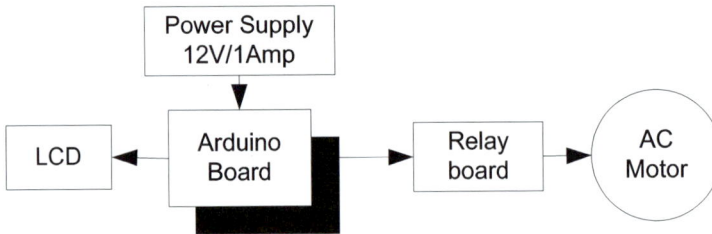

Fig. (5.16). Block diagram for the interfacing of AC motor with Arduino.

5.6.1. Circuit Diagram

Connect all the components to Arduino as per the connections as described-

1. RS pin of LCD is connected to pin12 of Arduino Uno.
2. RW pin of LCD is connected to GND pin of Arduino Uno.
3. RS pin of LCD is connected to pin11 of Arduino Uno.
4. D4 pin of LCD is connected to pin10 of Arduino Uno.
5. D5 pin of LCD is connected to pin9 of Arduino Uno.
6. D6 pin of LCD is connected to pin8 of Arduino Uno.

7. D7 pin of LCD is connected to pin7 of Arduino Uno.
8. Pins1 and 16 are connected to GND pin of power supply.
9. Pins 2 and 15 are connected to +5V pin of power supply.
10. +12V power supply jack is connected to DC jack of Arduino Uno.
11. AC motor ON/OF control is done through relay board. Input of relay board is connected to pin7 of Arduino Uno.
12. Relay board input pin is connected to collector of transistor 2N2222.
13. Emitter of transistor is connected to 'GND'.
14. Base of transistor is connected to pin 7 of the Arduino Uno trough transistor.
15. One terminal of AC source 220V is connected to common terminal of relay.
16. Other terminal of AC source is connected to one terminal of motor.
17. Other terminal of motor is connected to 'NO' pin of relay.

Fig. (**5.17**) shows circuit diagram for the interfacing of AC motor with Arduino.

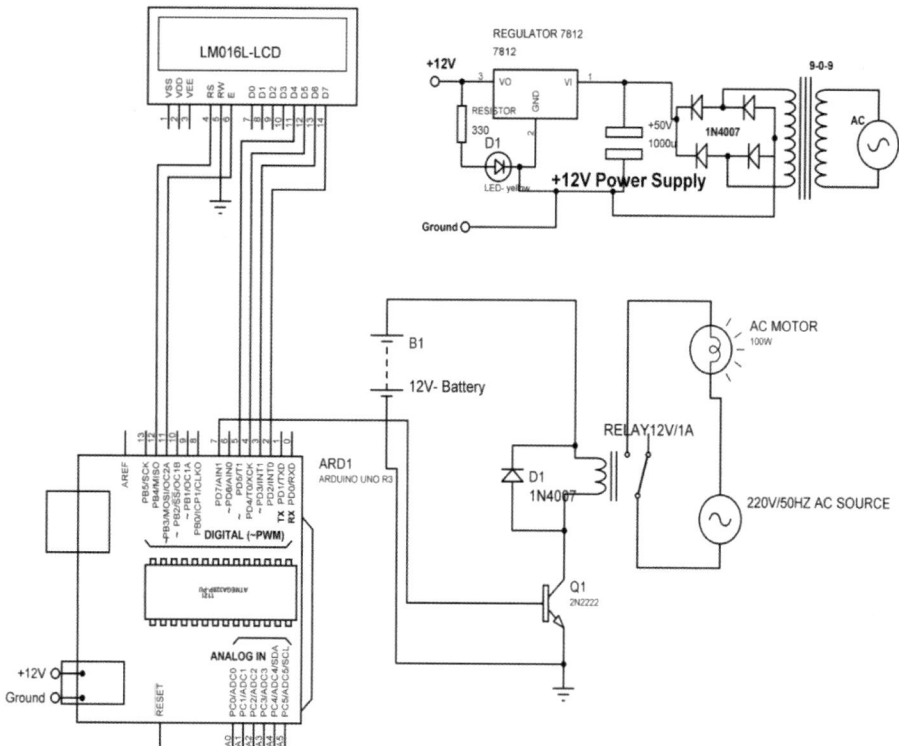

Fig. (5.17). Circuit diagram for the interfacing of AC motor with Arduino.

5.6.2. Program

#include <LiquidCrystal.h>

```
LiquidCrystal lcd(12, 11, 5, 4, 3, 2);

void setup()

{

lcd.begin(16, 2);// initialize the LCD

pinMode(9, OUTPUT);

lcd.print("AC MOTOR");

lcd.setCursor(0, 1);

lcd.print("control");

pinMode(7,OUTPUT)

delay(1000);

lcd.clear();

}

void loop()

{

digitalWrite(7,HIGH)

lcd.print("MOTOR ON");

delay(2000);

digitalWrite(7,LOW)

lcd.print("MOTOR OFF");

delay(2000);

}
```

5.6.3. Proteus Simulation Model

Connect the components with Arduino as described in section 5.6.1 in the virtual environment of Proteus simulator. Power supply need not to be connected in the virtual environment of Proteus. Load the program as described in section 5.6.2

and check the feasibility and working of the circuit. Fig. (**5.18**) shows the Proteus model for the system.

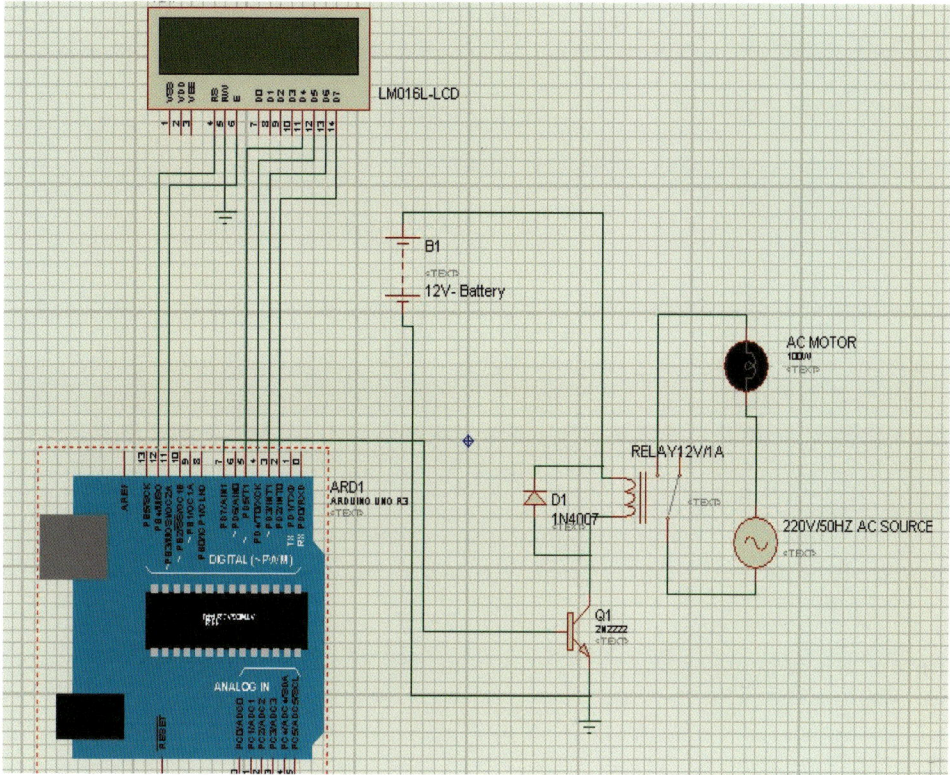

Fig. (5.18). Proteus simulation model of the Arduino interfacing with AC motor.

CHAPTER 6

Arduino Interfacing with Wireless Modems

Abstract: The wireless communication is technology in which information is communicated through air without cables from one device to other by using different modems like IR, RF, satellite *etc*. This chapter describes the wireless modem (XBee) used to communicate with programs and connecting examples.

Keywords: Arduino, XBee.

6.1. XBEE MODEM

XBee module communicates with protocol 802.15.4, which is a point-to-point communication protocol. It can be used to design WPAN with free band. It has range of 1600 meters in line of sight and 90 meters in indoors or urban area. It is used for embedded solutions providing addressable wireless end – point connectivity to devices. This XBee wireless device can be directly connected to the serial port (at 3.3 V) of the microcontroller.

Before it can be used in the system, it needs to be configured first. To configure XBee module please follow following steps-

6.1.1. Configuration of XBee

Step 1: Download X-CTU Software from link- https://www.digi.com/products/ xbee-rf-solutions/xctu-software/xctu#productsupport-utilities and install [XCTU v.6.3.10].

Fig. (**6.1**) shows DIGI XCTU software.

Fig. (6.1). DIGI XCTU.

Rajesh Singh, Anita Gehlot, Bhupendra Singh & Sushabhan Choudhury
All rights reserved-© 2018 Bentham Science Publishers

Fig. (**6.2**) shows XCTU starting Window.

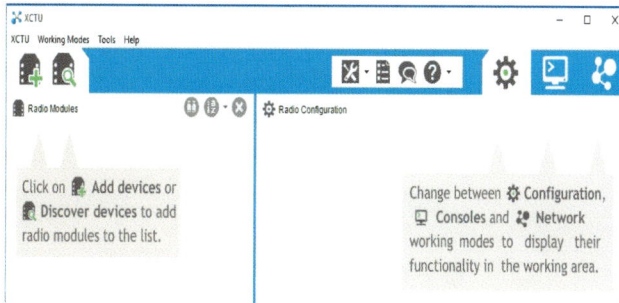

Fig. (6.2). XCTU starting Window.

Step 2: Connect two XBee board at same PC with two serial ports (COMPORT can be different for every PC), here XBee are connected at COM16 & COM8. Fig. (**6.3**) shows window after adding first XBee module at COM16.

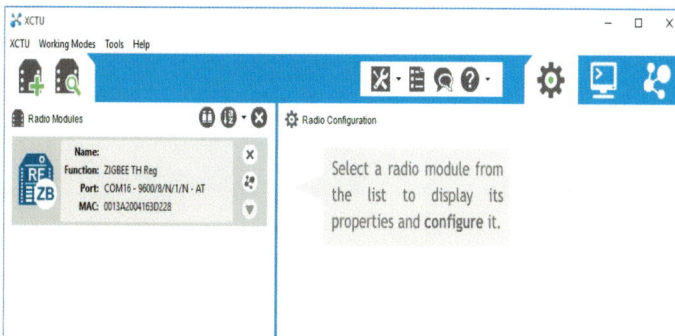

Fig. (6.3). Window after adding first XBee module at COM16.

Fig. (**6.4**) shows Window after adding second XBee module at COM8

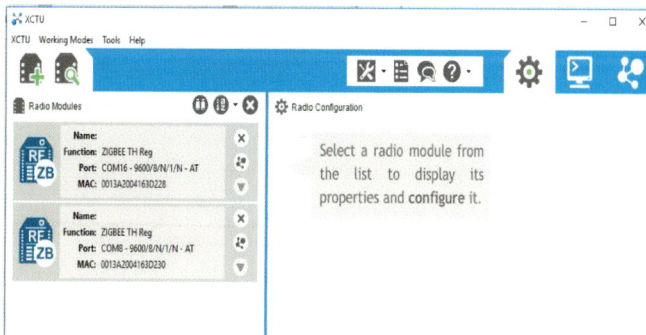

Fig. (6.4). Window after adding second XBee module at COM8.

Step 3: Configure 1st XBee as a coordinator.

Click XBee at COM16, the following settings will open.

Fig. (**6.5**) shows settings window.

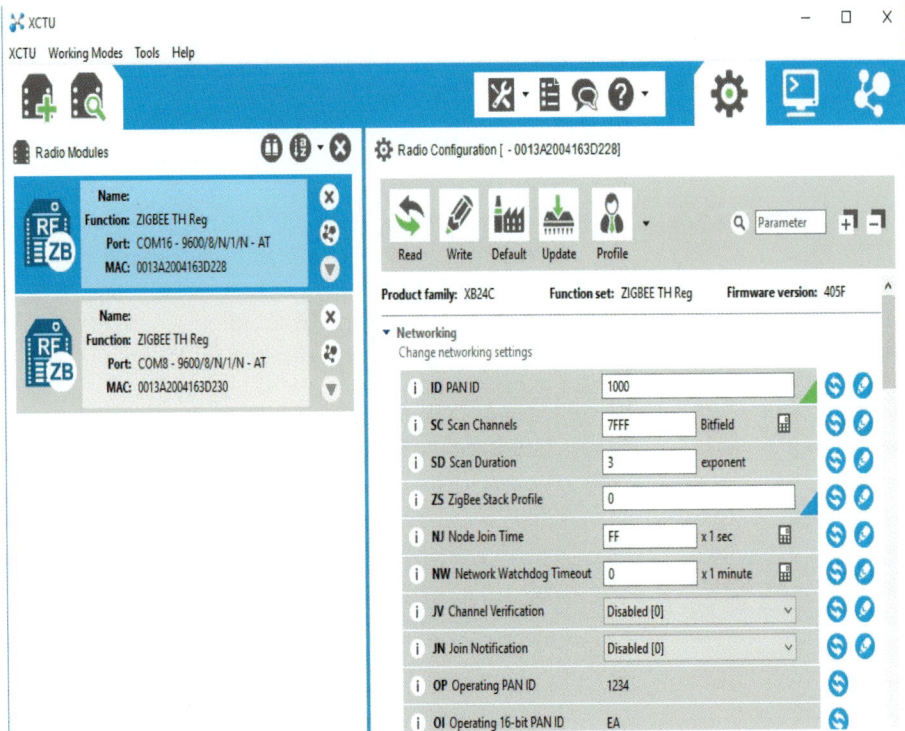

Fig. (6.5). Settings window.

To configure XBee as coordinator, settings are as follows-

PAN ID-1000

CE coordinator Enable=enabled [1]

DL destination address low=FFFF

Fig. (**6.6a**) shows configuring XBee as coordinator and Fig. (**6.6b**) shows snapshot of the setting for coordinator.

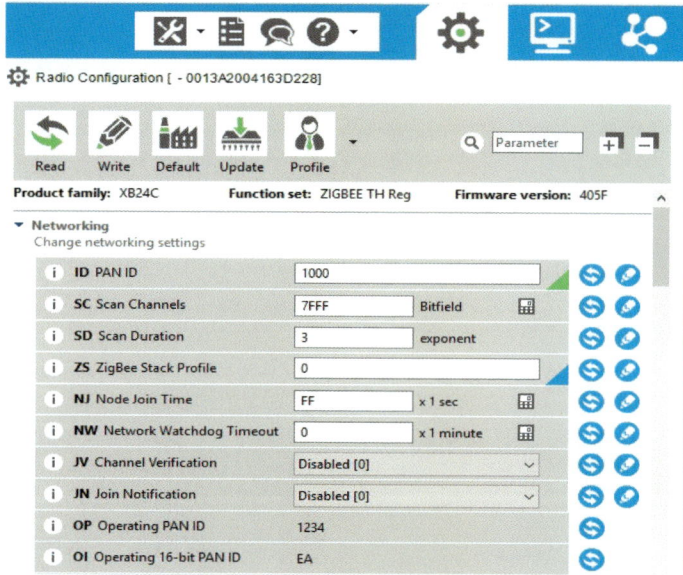

Fig. (6.6a). Configuring XBee as coordinator.

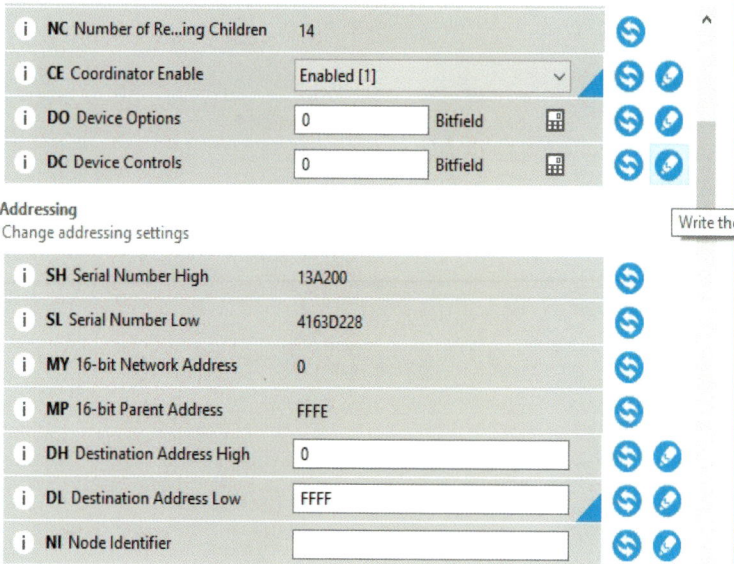

Fig. (6.6b). Snapshot of the Setting for coordinator.

Then click on write button to write the setting inside XBee [COM16]. Fig. (**6.7**) shows window to 'Click' on write button for COM16.

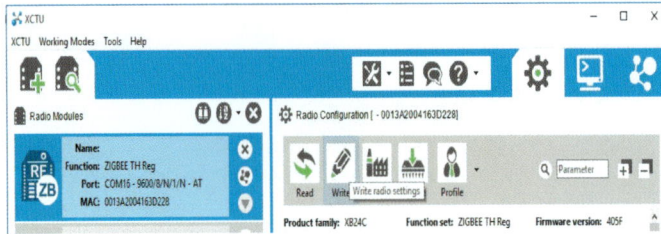

Fig. (6.7). Click on write button for COM16.

Step 4: Configure 2nd XBee as Router

Click XBee at COM8, the following settings will open.

Fig. (**6.8**) shows the settings window.

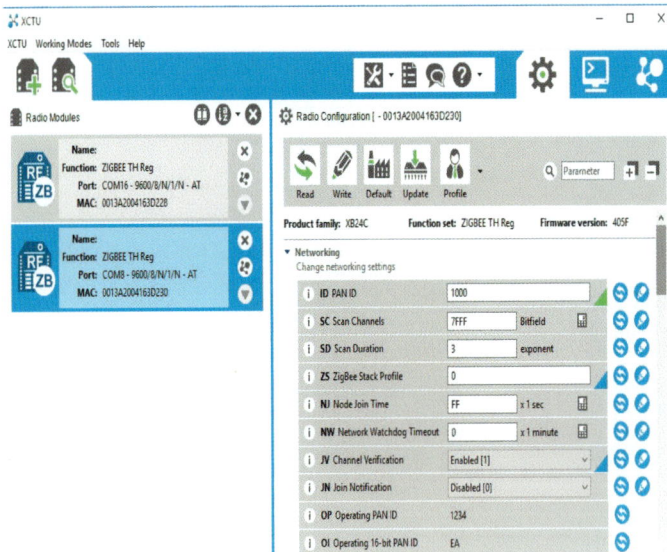

Fig. (6.8). Settings window.

To configure XBee as coordinator, settings are as follows:

PANID-1000

JV channel verification=Enabled[1]

CE coordinator Enable=Disabled[0]

DL destination address low=[0]

Fig. (**6.9a**) shows configuring XBee as Router and Fig. (**6.9b**) shows snapshot of the Setting for Router.

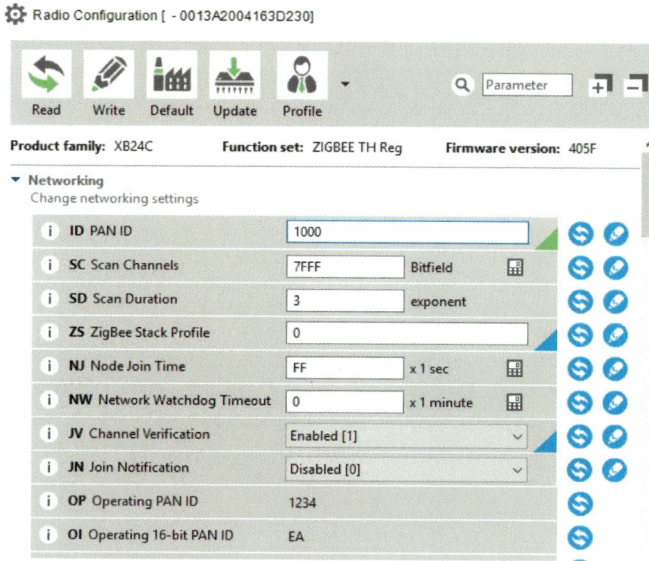

Fig. (6.9a). Configuring XBee as Router.

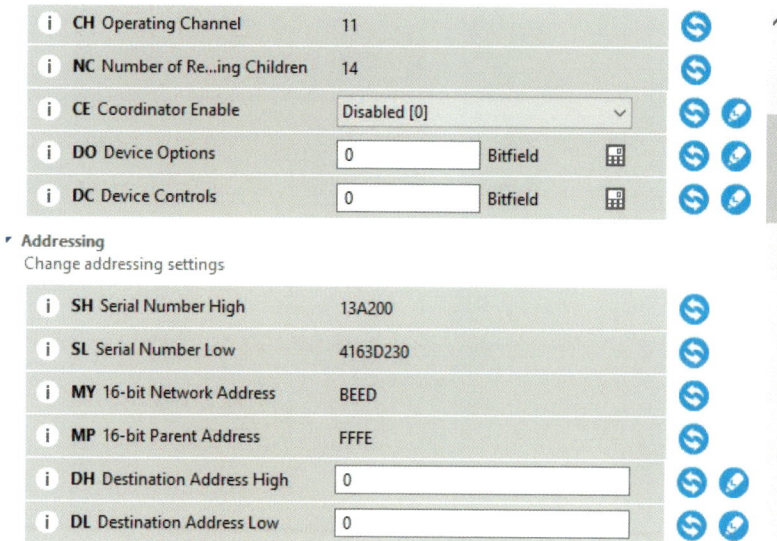

Fig. (6.9(b)). Snapshot of the Setting for Router.

Then click on write button to write the setting inside XBee [COM8]. Fig. (**6.10**) shows 'Click' on write button for COM8.

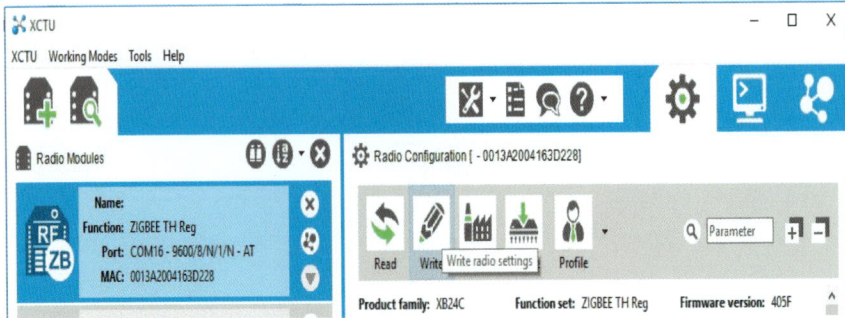

Fig. (6.10). Click on write button for COM8.

Step 5: Test the configuration

To check the communication between two XBee, open two different window for COM16 XBee and COM8 XBee. Fig. (**6.11**) shows two different window for both XBee and Fig. (**6.12**) shows communication between two XCTU.

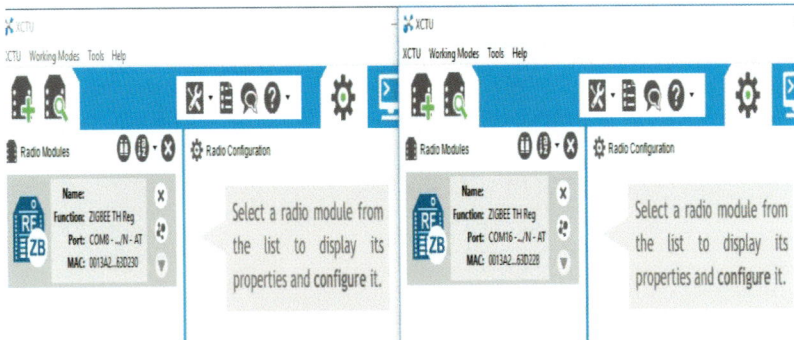

Fig. (6.11). Two different window for both XBee.

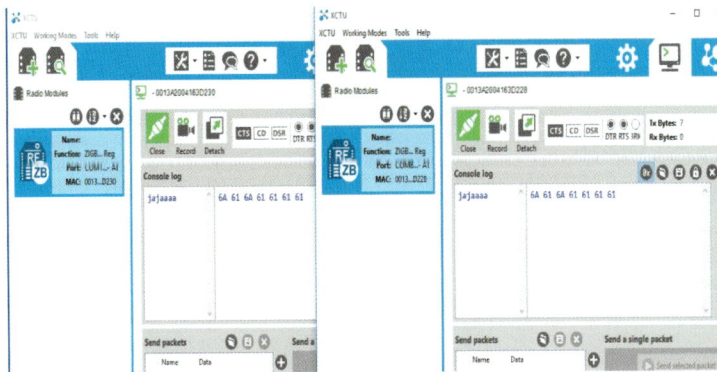

Fig. (6.12). Communication between two XCTU.

6.1.2. XBee Interfacing with Arduino

To understand the communication between two devices with XBee, the complete system is designed in two sections- transmitter and receiver. The transmitter is designed where the sensory data of LM35 is fetched from environment and transmitted through XBee. Receiver is designed to receive the data transmitted by transmitter. Fig. (**6.13**) shows the block diagram of the transmitter, comprises of Arduino, power supply, LM35, XBee. Fig. (**6.14**) shows the block diagram of receiver, comprises of Arduino and XBee.

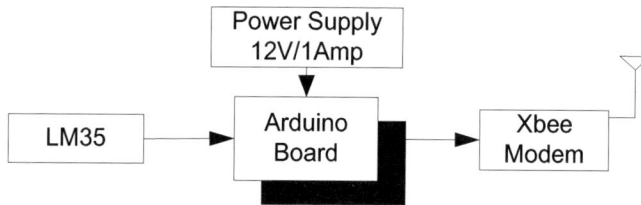

Fig. (6.13). Block diagram for XBee as transmitter.

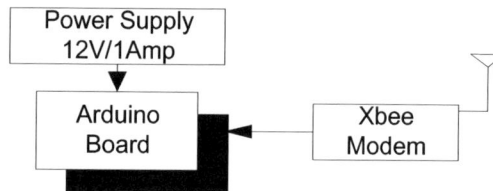

Fig. (6.14). Block diagram for XBee as receiver.

6.1.3. Circuit Diagram

Transmitter connection

1. RS pin of LCD is connected to pin12 of Arduino Uno.
2. RW pin of LCD is connected to GND pin of Arduino Uno.
3. RS pin of LCD is connected to pin11 of Arduino Uno.
4. D4 pin of LCD is connected to pin5 of Arduino Uno.
5. D5 pin of LCD is connected to pin4 of Arduino Uno.
6. D6 pin of LCD is connected to pin3 of Arduino Uno.
7. D7 pin of LCD is connected to pin2 of Arduino Uno.
8. Pins 1and 16 are connected to GND pin of power supply patch.
9. Pins 2 and 15 are connected to +5V pin of power supply patch.
10. Variable lag of 10K POT should be connected to pin 3 of LCD.
11. Two-fixed terminal should be connected to +5V and GND pin of patch.
12. +12V power supply jack is connected to DC jack of Arduino Uno.
13. Pins Rx and Tx of XBee are connected to pins Tx and Rx of Arduino Uno
14. +Vcc and GND of XBee are connected to +5V and GND of power supply.

Fig. (**6.15**) shows circuit diagram for XBee as transmitter [ROUTER].

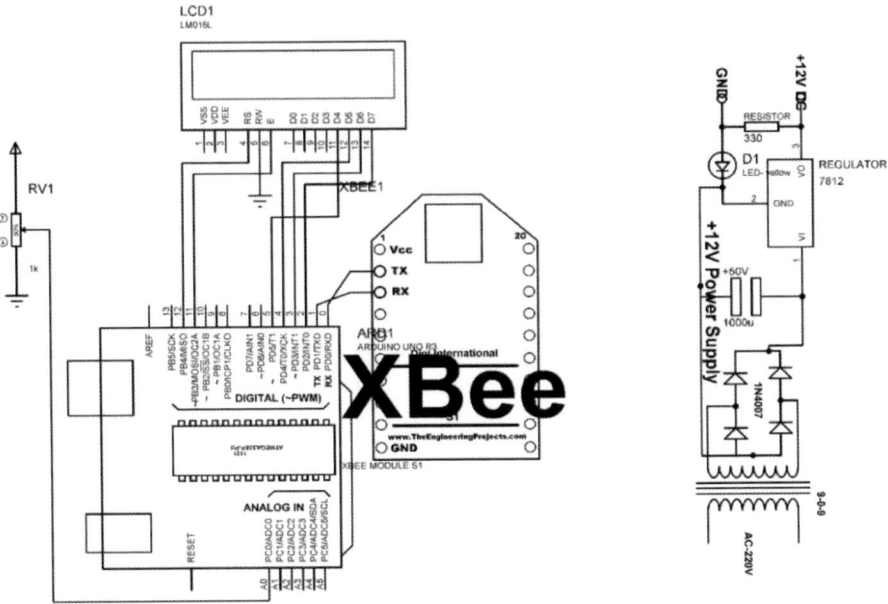

Fig. (6.15). Circuit diagram for XBee as transmitter [ROUTER].

Receiver connection

1. RS pin of LCD is connected to pin12 of Arduino Uno.
2. RW pin of LCD is connected to GND pin of Arduino Uno.
3. RS pin of LCD is connected to pin11 of Arduino Uno.
4. D4 pin of LCD is connected to pin5 of Arduino Uno.
5. D5 pin of LCD is connected to pin4 of Arduino Uno.
6. D6 pin of LCD is connected to pin3 of Arduino Uno.
7. D7 pin of LCD is connected to pin2 of Arduino Uno.
8. Pins 1and 16 are connected to GND pin of power supply patch.
9. Pins 2 and 15 are connected to +5V pin of power supply patch.
10. +12V power supply jack is connected to DC jack of Arduino Uno.
11. Pins Rx and Tx of XBee are connected to pins Tx and Rx of Arduino Uno.
12. +Vcc and GND of XBee are connected to +5V and GND of power supply.

Fig. (**6.16**) shows circuit diagram for XBee as receiver [COORDINATOR]

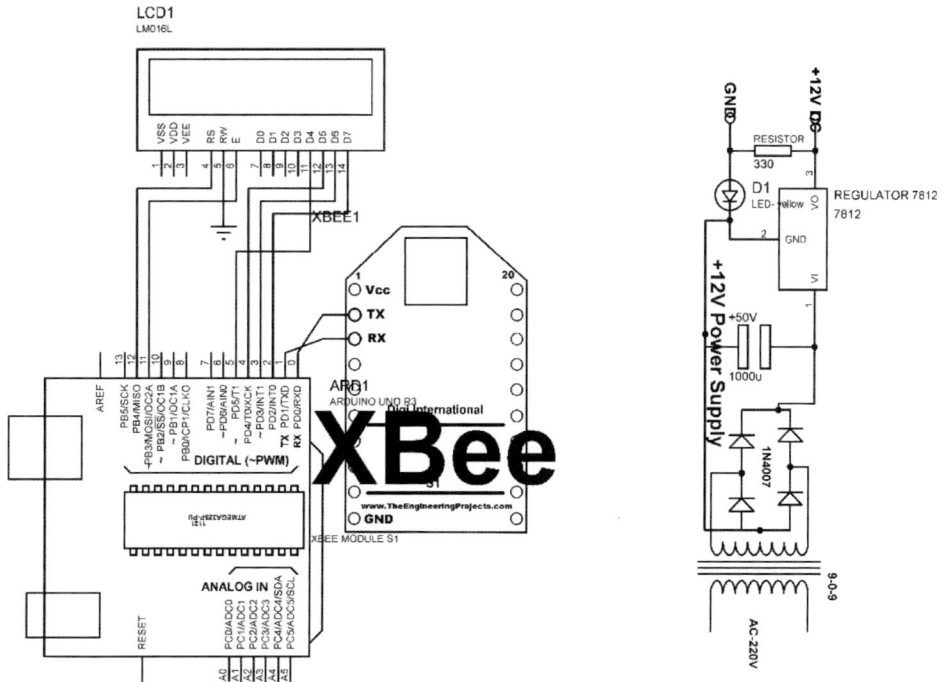

Fig. (6.16). Circuit diagram for XBee as receiver [COORDINATOR].

6.1.4. Program

Transmitter Program

#include <LiquidCrystal.h>

LiquidCrystal lcd(12, 11, 5, 4, 3, 2);

void setup()

{

lcd.begin(16,2);//initialse LCD

Serial.begin(9600);// Initialise serail baud rate 9600

lcd.setCursor(0,0);// set lcd cursor

lcd.print("XBee wireless");// display string on LCD

delay(2000);

```
}
void loop()
{
int VAL1 = analogRead(A0);// read analog pin
int FSR1=VAL1/2;// scale the VAL1
Serial.write(FSR1);// serial write FSR1 value
lcd.setCursor(0,0);// set lcd cursor
lcd.print("POT:");// display string on LCD
lcd.setCursor(0,1);//set lcd cursor
lcd.print(FSR1);//display int on LCD
delay(100); // delay 100ms
}
Receiver Program
#include <LiquidCrystal.h>
LiquidCrystal lcd(12, 11, 5, 4, 3, 2);
void setup()
{
lcd.begin(16,2);// initialise LCD
Serial.begin(9600);// initialise baud rate
lcd.setCursor(0,0);// set lcd cursor
lcd.print("XBee wireless");// display string on LCD
delay(2000);
}
void loop()
```

{

int XBee_Data=Serial.read();// read serial

Serial.print("XBee:");// print string serially

Serial.println(XBee_Data);//print int serially

lcd.setCursor(0,0);// set cursor

lcd.print("POT:");// print string on LCD

lcd.setCursor(0,1);// set cursor

lcd.print(XBee_Data);// print int on LCD

delay(100); // delay 100ms

}

6.1.5. Proteus Simulation Model

Connect the components with Arduino as described in section 6.1.3 in the virtual environment of Proteus simulator. Power supply need not to be connected in the virtual environment of Proteus. Load the program as described in section 6.1.4 and check the feasibility and working of the circuit. Fig. (**6.17**) shows the Proteus model for the system.

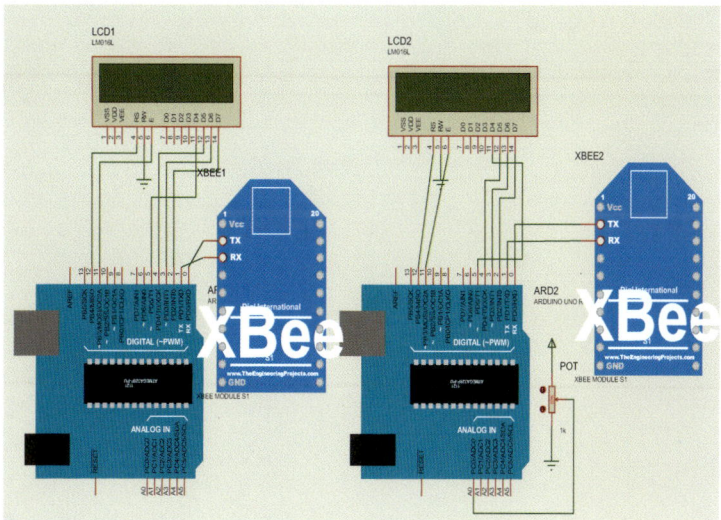

Fig. (6.17). Proteus simulation model of the Arduino interfacing with XBee.

CHAPTER 7

MATLAB GUI

Abstract: This chapter describes the steps to design MATLAB GUI. MATLAB is a programming language developed by MathWorks. It is used for, matrix manipulations, plotting of functions and data, implementation of algorithms and user interfaces. MATLAB applications include, signal processing and communications, Image and video processing, control systems, test and measurement, computational finance, computational biology *etc*.

Keywords: GUI, MATLAB.

7.1. GRAPHICAL USER INTERFACE (GUI)

It is a MATLAB tool that enables a user to perform interactive tasks.

GUI manipulates the commands that is given by the end user and responds accordingly. Each control and the GUI have one or more *callbacks* as command.

7.1.1. Steps to Create GUI in MATLAB

Step 1: Open GUI in MATLAB by clicking on icon shown in Fig. (**7.1**).

Fig. (7.1). Blank GUI MATLAB window.

Rajesh Singh, Anita Gehlot, Bhupendra Singh & Sushabhan Choudhury
All rights reserved-© 2018 Bentham Science Publishers

Step 2: Click on OK button then the window as shown in Fig. (**7.2**) will be opened.

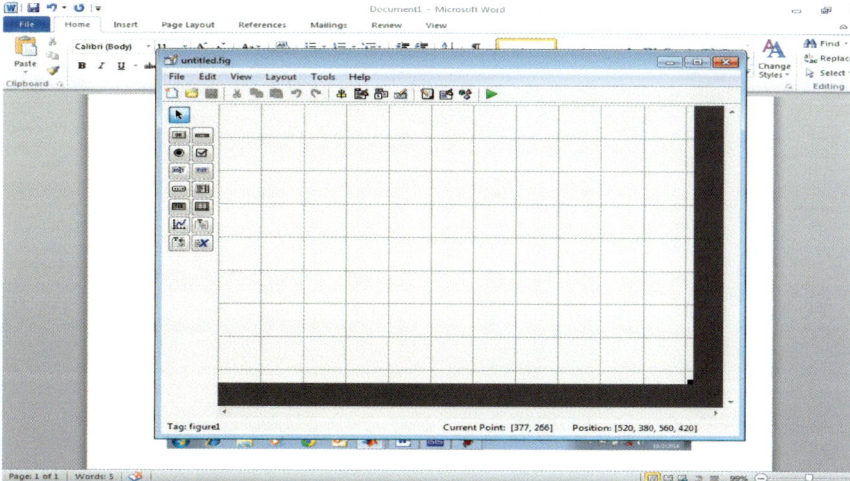

Fig. (7.2). GUI window.

Step 3: Click on the push button to select two push buttons and draw on the GUI window as shown in Fig. (**7.3**).

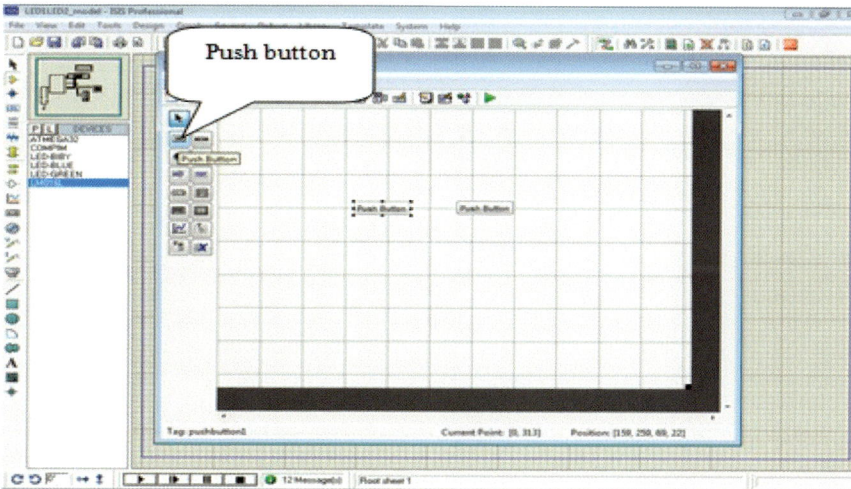

Fig. (7.3). Push buttons on GUI.

Step 4: Double click on push button will open the window as shown in Fig. (**7.4**), where some options like- Font size, color and name can be assigned, then save it and repeat it for another push button. Let's say button name as 'A' and font size-10.

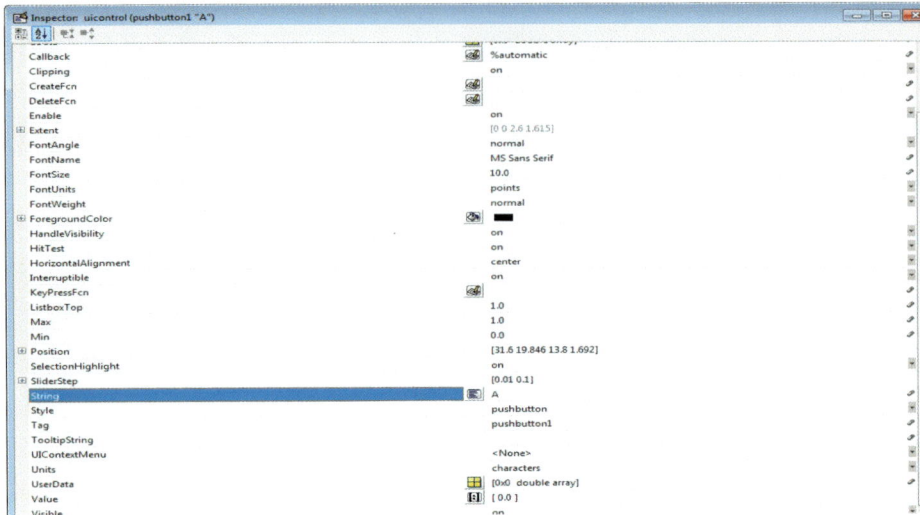

Fig. (7.4). Window to configure the push button.

Step 5: Right click on 'A' button then go to view callbacks to callback as shown in Fig. (**7.5**).

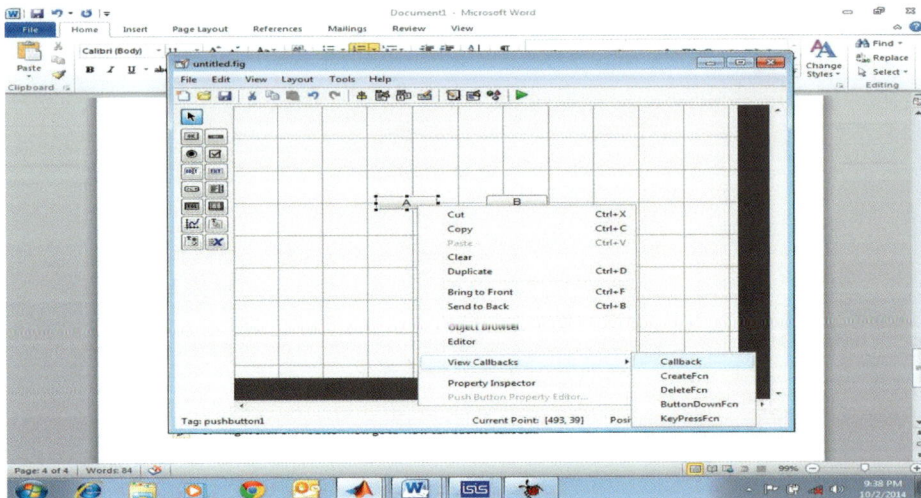

Fig. (7.5). Window to go for callback.

Step 6: Click on callback and save the given GUI by any name. Then it will open the new window with function name [function pushbutton1_Callback(hObject, eventdata, handles)].

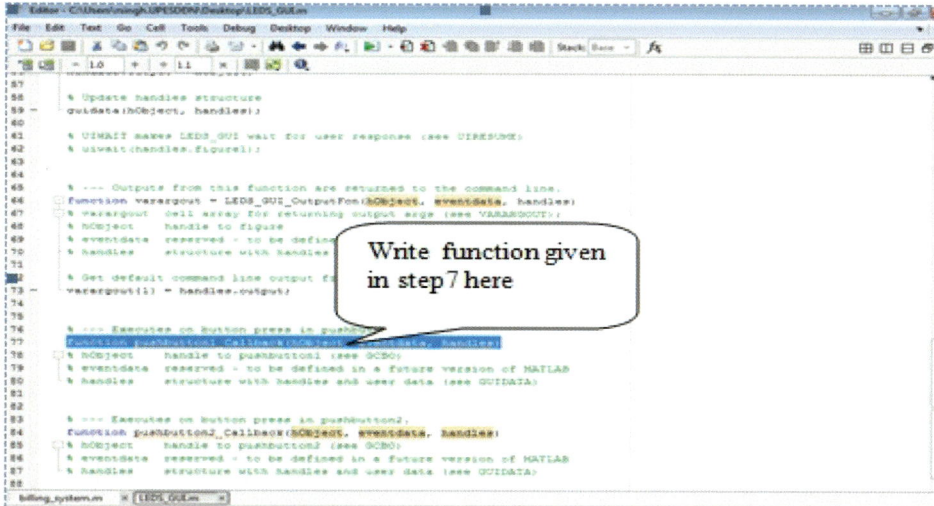

Fig. (7.6). Window with function name.

Step 7: Write the Function inside window shown in Fig. (**7.6**) to open the COM port and data command.

The Function for push button 'A' is as follows as shown in Fig. (7.7)

% --- Executes on button press in pushbutton2.

function pushbutton1_Callback(hObject, eventdata, handles)

% hObject handle to pushbutton1 (see GCBO)

% eventdata reserved to be defined in a future version of MATLAB

% handles structure with handles and user data (see GUIDATA)

clear all;

s=serial('COM1');

set(s,'BaudRate',9600);

fopen(s);

```
fprintf(s,'%s','a');

fclose(s)

delete(s)

clear s
```

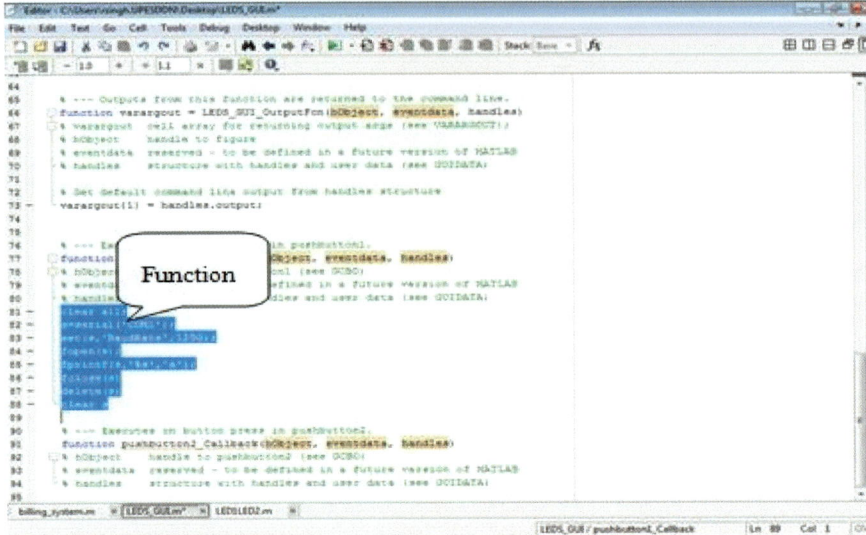

Fig. (7.7). Function for push button 'A'.

Step 8: Repeat the same process for push button 'B' as shown in Fig. **(7.8)**

```
% --- Executes on button press in pushbutton 'B'

function pushbutton2_Callback(hObject, eventdata, handles)

% hObject handle to pushbutton2 (see GCBO)

% eventdata reserved to be defined in a future version of MATLAB

% handles structure with handles and user data (see GUIDATA)

clear all;

s=serial('COM1');

set(s,'BaudRate',9600);

fopen(s);
```

fprintf(s,'%s','b');

fclose(s)

delete(s)

clear s

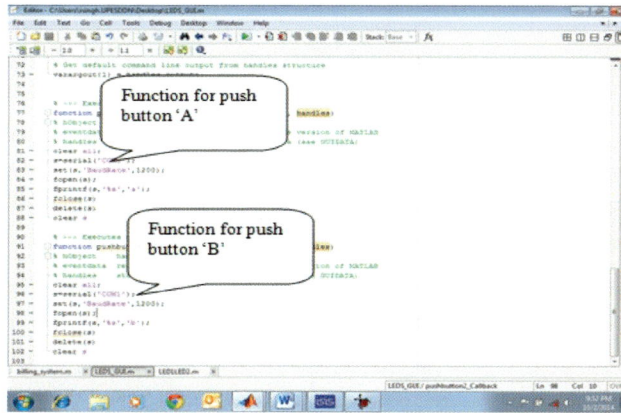

Fig. (7.8). function for push button 'B'.

Note: By this method any button or module can be configured, available in GUI of MATLAB.

Step 9: Resize the GUI by dragging the Black point on window as shown in Fig. (**7.9**).

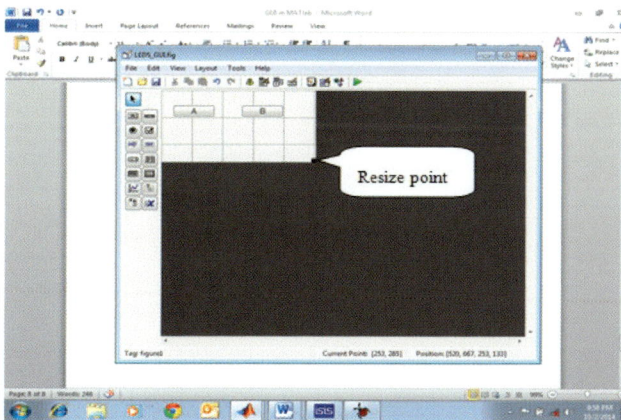

Fig. (7.9). Resize the GUI window.

Step 10: Run the GUI by clicking on Green button. The untitled window will appear which is used to run the model as shown in Fig. (**7.10**).

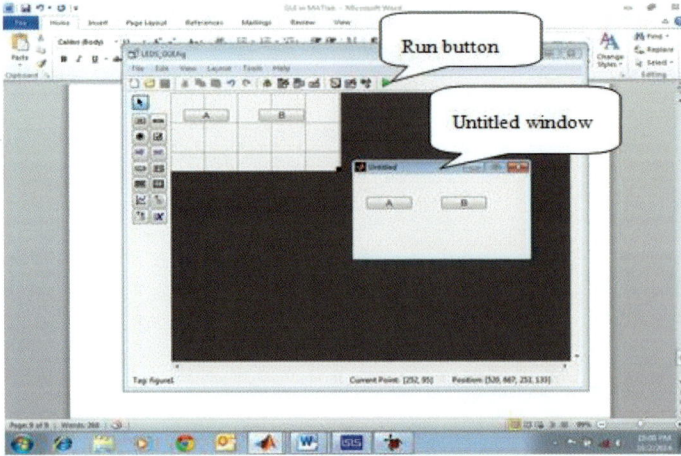

Fig. (7.10). Run command window for GUI.

CHAPTER 8

Simulink and Arduino I/O Package

Abstract: Arduino I/O package from Mathworks provides an interface between Simulink and hardware system. It allows real time communication between Arduino and MATLAB. It needs a simple program to load in Arduino and create Simulink by simple steps. The program acts a server for communicating the information from input devices, Arduino and Simulink model with special blocks and commands.

In this case Arduino will not run separate program to control the devices rather run the executable program from Simulink.

Keywords: Arduino I/O package, Simulink.

8.1. GET STARTED WITH SIMULINK ARDUINO I/O PACKAGE

To get started with Simulink and Arduino I/O package, following components are required.

Component Requirement-

1. Arduino (Mega2560 or UNO).
2. MATLAB 2013 (or above).
3. Installed Arduino package in Simulink.
4. Arduino USB cable (for communication).

8.1.1. Steps to Install Arduino I/O Package in MATLAB

MATLAB Simulink don't come with pre-installed packages for Arduino.

1. Download it from the official website of Mathworks. For MATLAB 2013 and above versions.
2. Run the MATLAB program
3. Go to the *HOME* menu, in menu bar
4. Go to option of ad-Ons in the block of *RESOURCES*
5. 'Click' on 'get hardware support packages'
6. On clicking 'support Package', Installer window will open

Rajesh Singh, Anita Gehlot, Bhupendra Singh & Sushabhan Choudhury
All rights reserved-© 2018 Bentham Science Publishers

This window will have following options-

    a. Install from internet.
    b. Download from internet.
    c. Install from folder.
    d. Uninstall.

Install package from where you want to.

7. Support package can be installed by writing target installer in command window.
    1. 'Click' *Next* on that Support Package installer window in bottom right.
    2. All the available hardware support packages will be shown in Next window.
    3. 'Click' on '*Arduino*' and 'click' *Next.*
    4. *Sign in to* Mathworks account, if don't have create it with working email address.
    5. Login and click next and next and it will take a little time to download and install. Then 'click' finish.
    6. Now install this package.

8.1.2. Making Arduino Compatible with MATLAB

Follow the steps as below for making Arduino compatible with MATLAB.

1. Arduino IO package will download by folder name 'ArduinoIO'
2. Connect Arduino board with the computer using its data cable.
3. Open this folder, one folder by name of 'pde' will be there.
4. Open this folder and then open the Arduino program in folder 'ADIOES'.

Fig. (**8.1**) shows the ADIOES program to load to Arduino to work with IO package.

1. Burn this program in the Arduino.
2. Now Arduino is compatible with Simulink and model created in it.

8.1.3. Creating Model in Simulink

To create a Simulink model, go to Simulink menu, 'Click' on the Simulink Library and then open ArduinoIO library. There are blocks available to use according to the requirement of the project. Mainly two types of blocks- read blocks and write blocks.

```
adioes | Arduino 1.6.4

File  Edit  Sketch  Tools  Help

  adioes

/* Analog and Digital Input and Output Server for MATLAB      */
/* Giapiero Campa, Copyright 2012 The MathWorks, Inc          */

/* This file is meant to be used with the MATLAB arduino IO
     package, however, it can be used from the IDE environment
      (or any other serial terminal) by typing commands like:

    0e0 :  assigns digital pin  #4  (e)  as  input
    0f1 :  assigns digital pin  #5  (f)  as  output
    0n1 :  assigns digital pin  #13 (n)  as  output

    1c  :  reads digital pin  #2  (c)
    1e  :  reads digital pin  #4  (e)
    2n0 :  sets digital pin  #13 (n)  low
    2n1 :  sets digital pin  #13 (n)  high
    2f1 :  sets digital pin  #5  (f)  high
    2f0 :  sets digital pin  #5  (f)  low
    4j2 :  sets digital pin  #9  (f)  to   50=ascii (2) over 255

                                                    1       Arduino Uno on COM3
```

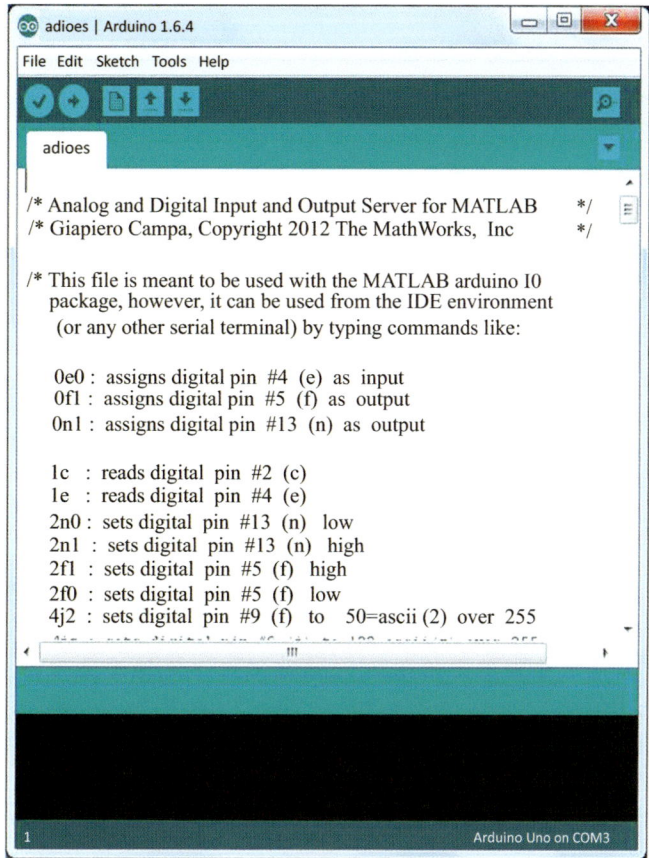

Fig. (8.1). ADIOES program to load to Arduino to work with IO package.

8.2. READ BLOCKS

These blocks takes the information from input pin or communicate the real time data to the Simulink.

8.3. WRITE BLOCKS

These blocks are to communicate Simulink data to the outer world.

Simulink model can be designed by connecting the blocks from library to the blank space provided to create model. Build the Simulink model & run on hardware to communicate with outer world.

CHAPTER 9

Digital Read/Write and Analog Read/Write with Arduino I/O Package

Abstract: This chapter describes about the examples of digital read/write and analog read/write with Arduino I/O package, its designing process and working.

Keywords: Analog read/write, Arduino I/O Package, Arduino, Digital read/write.

9.1. DIGITAL READ/WRITE

To understand the digital read/write with Arduino I/O package, let's take example of making LED 'ON/OFF' with a button. Fig. (**9.1**) shows the block diagram for the system, which comprises of Arduino board, a switch or button, LED (connected to Arduino through resistor).

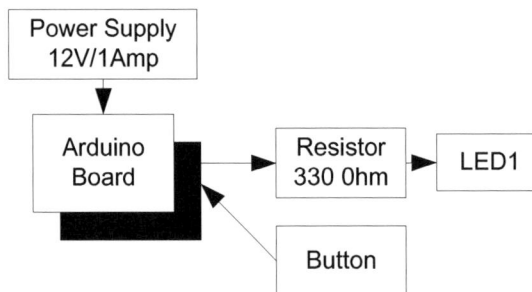

Fig. (9.1). Block diagram for digital read/write.

9.1.1. Circuit Diagram

Connect all the components to Arduino as per the connections as described-

1. Push Button or switch is connected at pin8 of Arduino Uno.
2. LED indicator at connected to pin7 of Arduino Uno through 330 ohm of resistor.
3. DC jack of +12 V power supply is connected to power supply DC jack of Arduino mega.

Rajesh Singh, Anita Gehlot, Bhupendra Singh & Sushabhan Choudhury
All rights reserved-© 2018 Bentham Science Publishers

Fig. (**9.2**) shows circuit diagram for the system.

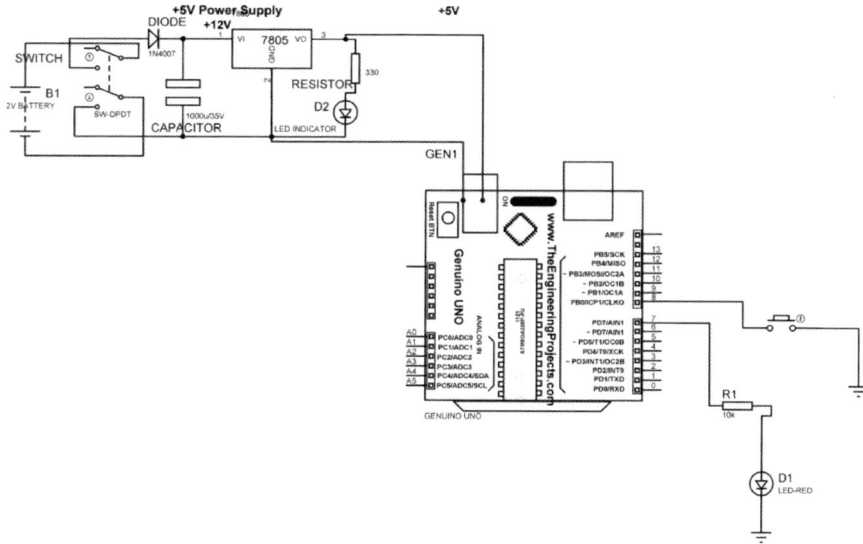

Fig. (9.2). Circuit diagram for digital read/write.

9.1.2. Simulink Model

Connect the required blocks for the system in Simulink space and burn the specified program for ADIOES to Arduino and check the working of the system. Fig. (**9.3**) shows simulink model for digital read/write.

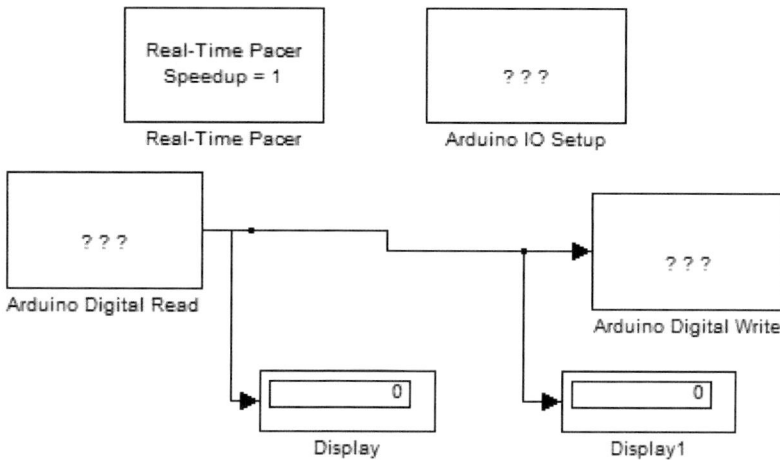

Fig. (9.3). Simulink model for digital read/write.

9.2. ANALOG READ/WRITE

To understand the analog read/write with Arduino I/O package, let's take example of making LED 'ON/OFF' with a POT. Fig. (9.4) shows the block diagram for the system, which comprises of Arduino board, a POT, LED (connected to Arduino through resistor).

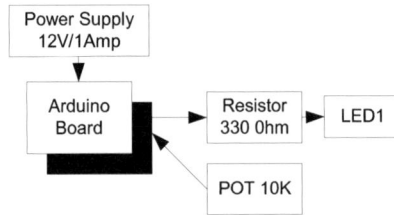

Fig. (9.4). Block diagram for analog read/write.

9.2.1. Circuit Diagram

Connect all the components to Arduino as per the connections as described:

1. Variable terminal of POT is attached at A0 analog pin of Arduino Uno.
2. Fixed two terminals of POT is connected to +5V and GND of power supply extension/explorer.
3. LED indicator at connected to pin 3 of Arduino Uno through 330 ohm of resistor.
4. DC jack of +12 V power supply is connected to power supply DC jack of Arduino mega.

Fig. (**9.5**) shows circuit diagram for analog read/write.

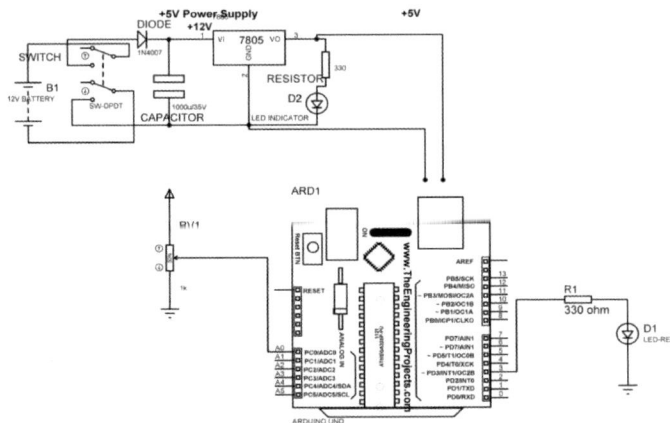

Fig. (9.5). Circuit diagram for analog read/write.

9.2.2. Simulink Model

Connect the required blocks as discussed in chapter 7 & 8 for the system in Simulink space and burn the specified program for ADIOES to Arduino and check the working of the system. Fig. (**9.6**) shows simulink model for analog read/write.

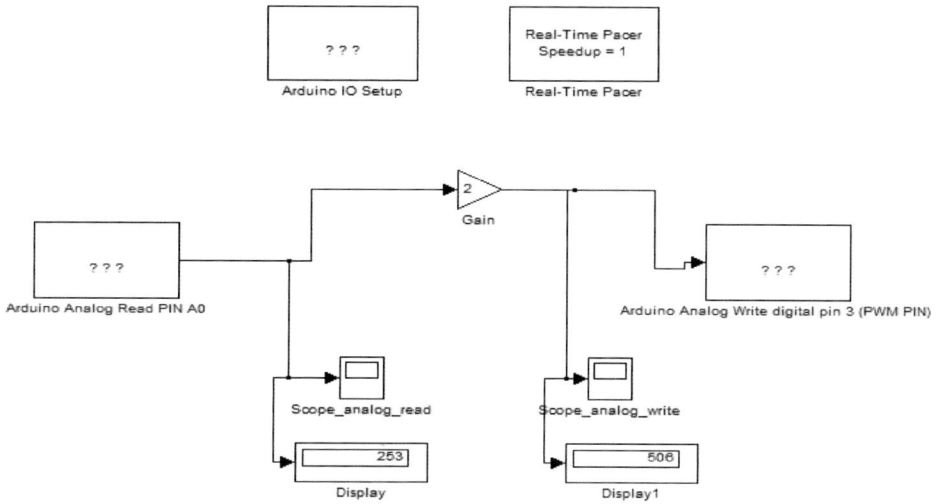

Fig. (9.6). Simulink model for analog read/write.

CHAPTER 10

Digital Read with Proximity and Touch Sensor and Digital Write on LED with Arduino I/O Package

Abstract: This chapter describes the process for digital read and digital write with Arduino I/O package, with the help of proximity a & touch sensor and LED.

Keywords: Arduino, Digital read, Digital write.

The system comprises of Arduino board, two LED, proximity sensor, touch sensor and power supply. Fig. (**10.1**) shows the block diagram for the system

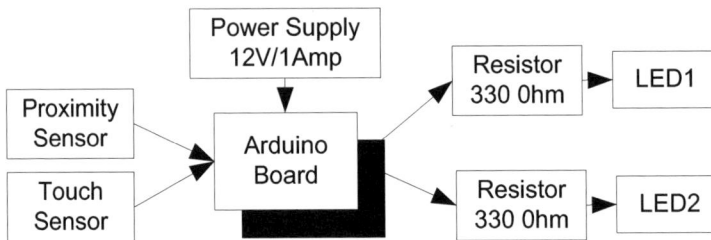

Fig.(10.1). Block diagram of system.

10.1. CIRCUIT DIAGRAM

Connect all the components to Arduino as per the connections as described-

1. Touch sensor OUT pin is connected to 7 pin of Arduino mega.
2. Proximity sensor OUT pin is connected to 6pin of Arduino mega.
3. LED D1 is connected with 8 pin of Arduino mega which is indicator to touch sensor through 330 ohm resistor.
4. LED D2 is connected with 8 pin of Arduino mega which is indicator to proximity sensor through 330 ohm resistor.
5. +Vcc and Ground pin of individual sensors is connected to +5V and GND pin of power Patch/explorer.
6. DC jack of +12 V power supply is connected to power supply DC jack of Arduino mega.

Rajesh Singh, Anita Gehlot, Bhupendra Singh & Sushabhan Choudhury
All rights reserved-© 2018 Bentham Science Publishers

Fig. (**10.2**) shows circuit diagram for the system.

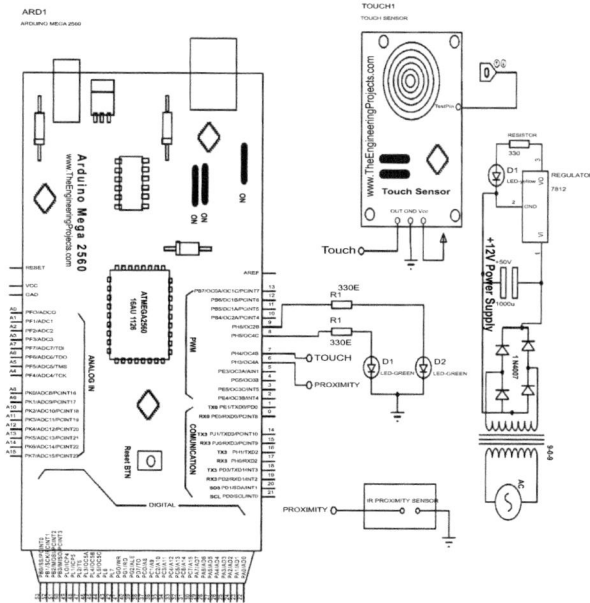

Fig. (10.2). Circuit diagram for the system.

10.2. SIMULINK MODEL

Follow the steps defined in chapter 8 and design the Simulink model. Burn the predefined I/O program in Arduino and see the results on oscilloscope. Figs. (**10.3**) & (**10.4**) shows the Simulink model for the system.

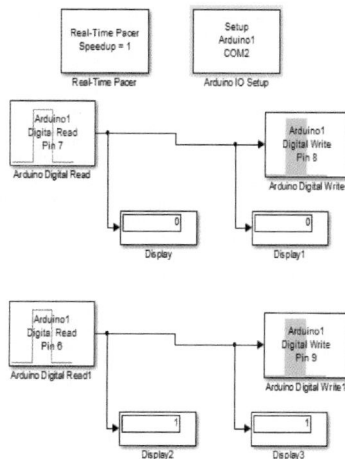

Fig. (10.3). Simulink Model 1.

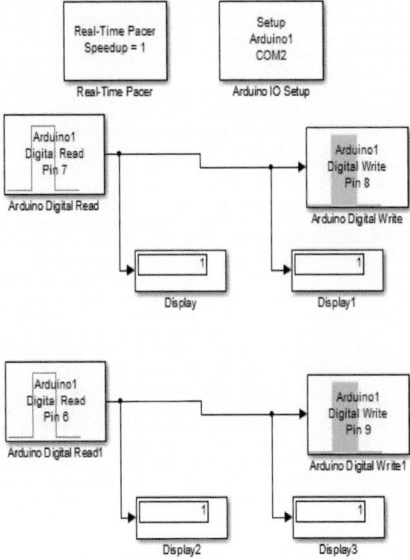

Fig. (10.4). Simulink Model 2.

CHAPTER 11

Key Touch Sensor Based Home Automation with Arduino I/O Package

Abstract: This chapter describes the home automation system with Arduino I/O package and MATLAB Simulink for monitoring the status of the appliances. The system comprises of Arduino board (connected to MATLAB through serial), four home appliances (Bulb1, Fan1, Bulb2, Fan2) which are connected to Arduino through transistor and relay, and power supply. The system is designed to control appliances with touch sensor.

Keywords: Arduino, Bulb, Fan, Home automation, Key touch sensor.

Fig. (**11.1**) shows the block diagram for the system which comprises of Arduino board (connected to MATLAB through serial), four home appliances (Bulb1, Fan1, Bulb2, Fan2) which are connected to Arduino through transistor and relay, and power supply.

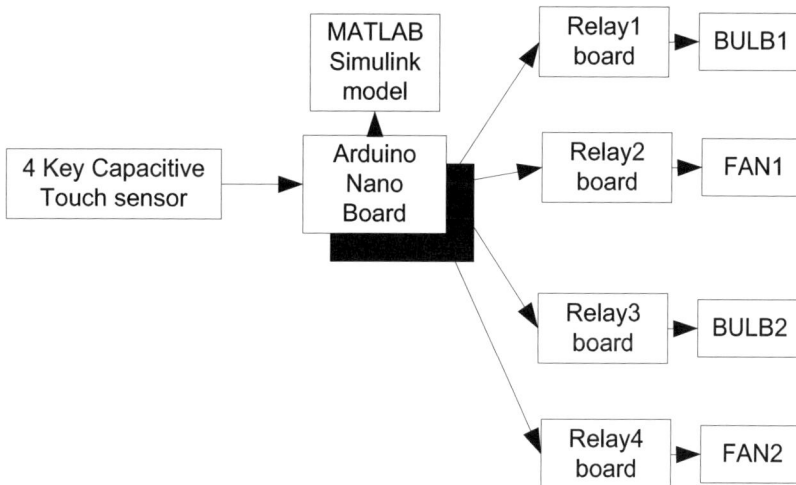

Fig. (11.1). Block diagram for home automation system.

Rajesh Singh, Anita Gehlot, Bhupendra Singh & Sushabhan Choudhury
All rights reserved-© 2018 Bentham Science Publishers

11.1. CIRCUIT DIAGRAM

Connect all the components to Arduino as per the connections as described-

1. 4 key Touch sensor OUT1 pin is connected to 7 pin of Arduino nano.
2. 4 key Touch sensor OUT2 pin is connected to 6 pin of Arduino nano.
3. 4 key Touch sensor OUT3 pin is connected to 5 pin of Arduino nano.
4. 4 key Touch sensor OUT4 pin is connected to 4 pin of Arduino nano.
5. First appliance is connected with 12 pin of Arduino nano which is indicator to touch sensor through 330 ohm resistor.
6. Second appliance is connected with 11 pin of Arduino nano.
7. third appliance is connected with 10 pin of Arduino nano.
8. forth appliance is connected with 9 pin of Arduino nano.
9. +Vcc and Ground pin of sensor is connected to +5V and GND pin of power Patch/explorer.
10. DC jack of +12 V power supply is connected to power supply DC jack of Arduino nano.

Fig. (**11.2**) shows circuit diagram for home automation system.

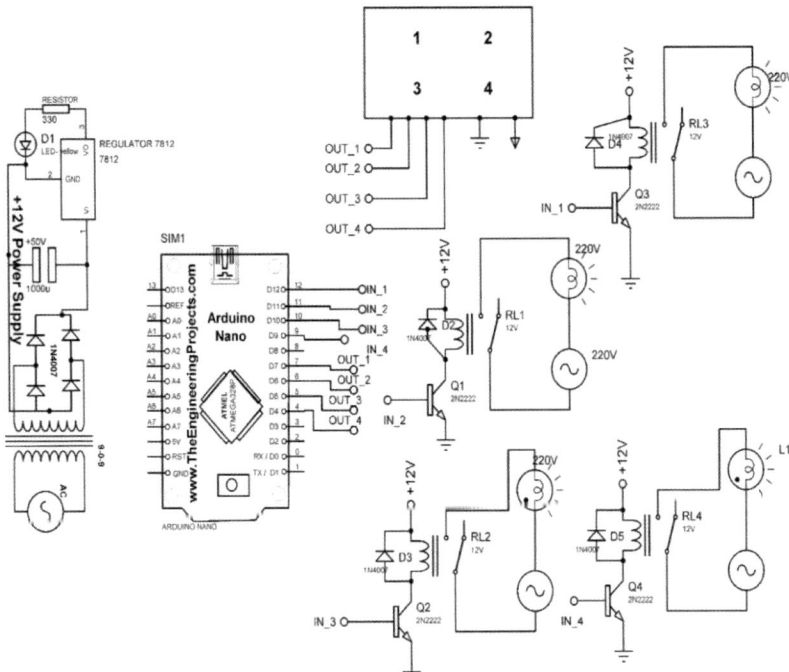

Fig. (11.2). Circuit diagram for home automation system.

11.2. SIMULINK MODEL

Connect the required blocks as discussed in chapter 7 & 8 for the system in Simulink space and burn the specified program for ADIOES to Arduino and check the working of the system. Fig. (**11.3**) shows the simulink model for the system.

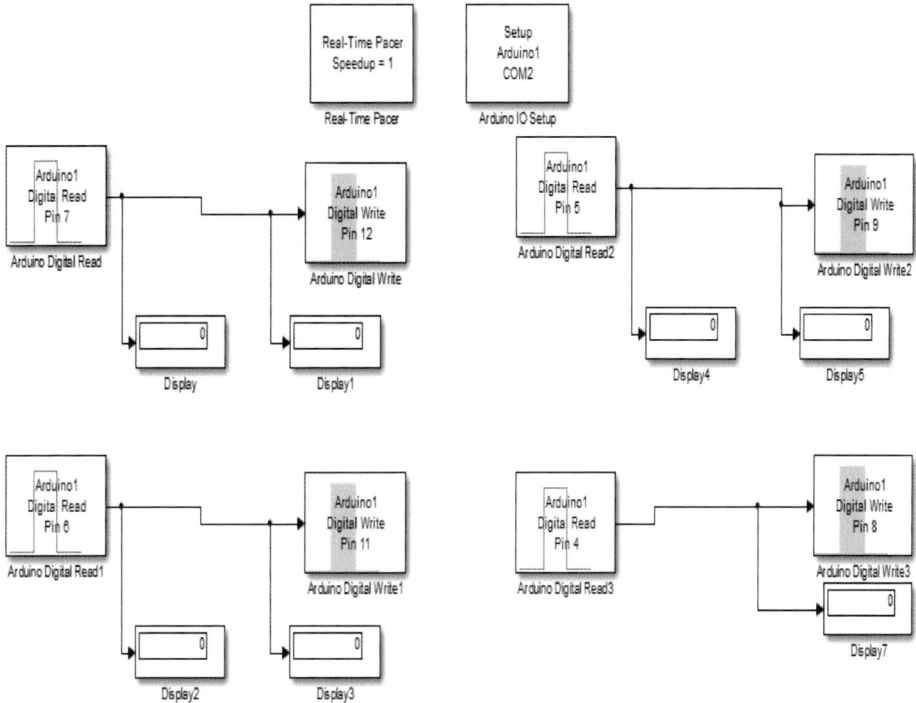

Fig. (11.3). Simulink Model.

CHAPTER 12

Sun Tracker System Using LDR with Arduino I/O Package

Abstract: A sun tracker is a device that orients PV panel towards the sun, to maximize the energy efficiency of the system. Sun trackers are designed to enhance the power generation capacity of solar panels. In this chapter Arduino based sun tracker system is designed. Sun intensity is measured with the help of light dependent resistor (LDR), placed at PV panels. The system comprises of the Arduino board, three LDR and servo motor. Servo motor is connected to orient the PV panels in such a way that PV panel is always perpendicular to the sun rays to generate maximum energy.

Keywords: Arduino, LDR, PV panel, Sun tracker system.

Fig. (**12.1**) shows the block diagram of the system. It comprises of the Arduino board, three LDR and servo motor.

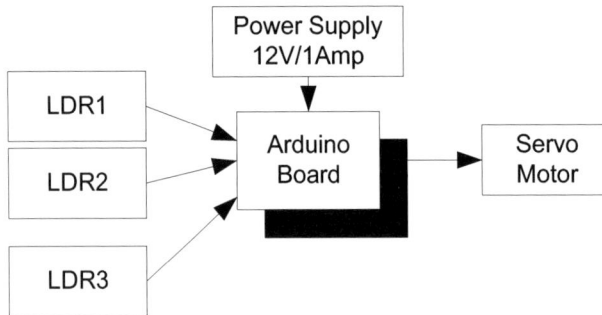

Fig. (12.1). Block diagram for the sun tracking system.

12.1. CIRCUIT DIAGRAM

Connect all the components to Arduino as per the connections as described-

1. LDR sensor1 analog out pin is connected to A0 pin of Arduino Uno.
2. LDR sensor2 analog out pin is connected to A1 pin of Arduino Uno.
3. LDR sensor3 analog out pin is connected to A2 pin of Arduino Uno.

Rajesh Singh, Anita Gehlot, Bhupendra Singh & Sushabhan Choudhury
All rights reserved-© 2018 Bentham Science Publishers

4. +Vcc and Ground pin of individual sensors is connected to +5V and GND pin of power Patch/explorer.

5. DC jack of +12 V power supply is connected to power supply DC jack of Arduino mega.

6. Servo motor PWM in pin is connected to pin 3 of Arduino Uno.

Fig. (**12.2**) shows circuit diagram for the sun tracking system.

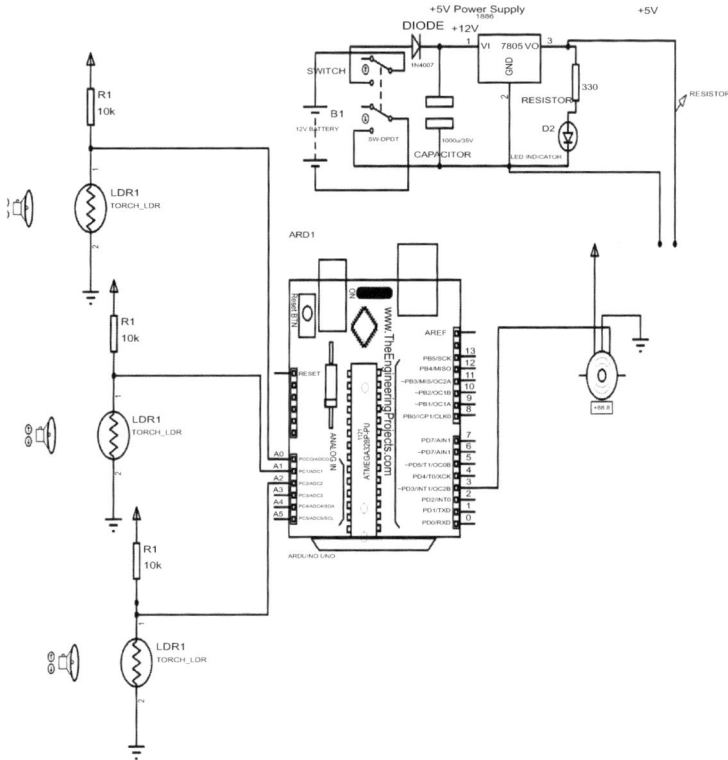

Fig. (12.2). Circuit diagram for the sun tracking system.

12.2. SIMULINK MODEL

Connect the required blocks for the system in Simulink space and burn the specified program for ADIOES to Arduino and check the working of the system. Fig. (**12.3**) shows simulink model for the system.

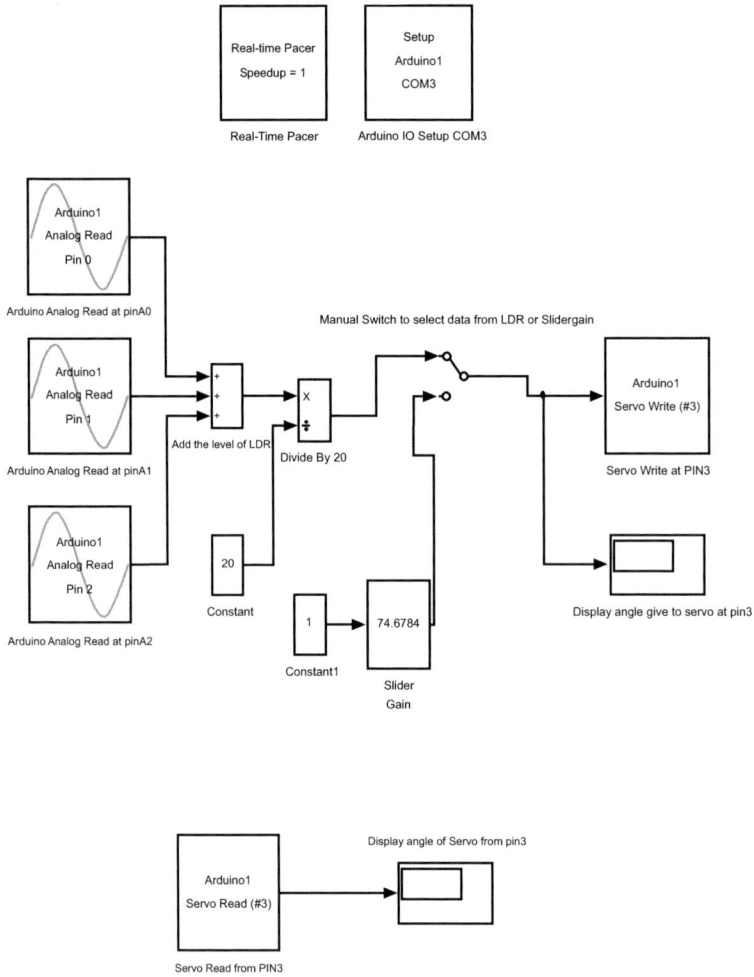

Fig. (12.3). Simulink Model for the system.

CHAPTER 13

Robot Control and Sensor Data Acquisition System with Arduino I/O Package

Abstract: This chapter describes the control of robot and sensory data acquisition system with Arduino I/O package. The system comprises of Arduino board, LM35, POT, L293D, DC motors, power supply. DC motors are used to move the robot in 'forward' 'reverse' 'left' and 'right'.

Keywords: Arduino, Arduino I/O Package, Data Acquisition, Robot Control.

Fig. (**13.1**) shows the block diagram of the system, comprises of Arduino board, LM35, POT, L293D, DC motors, power supply.

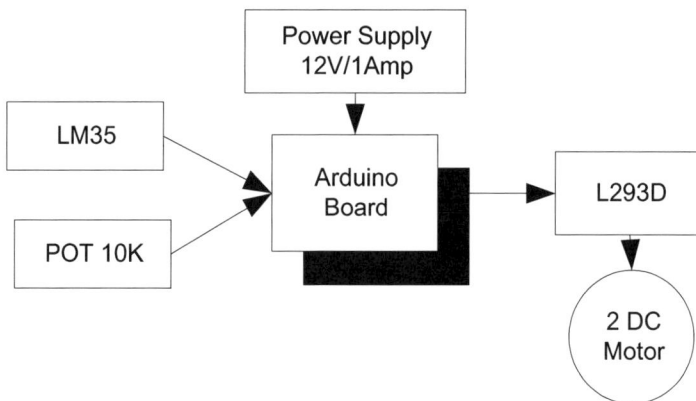

Fig. (13.1). Block diagram for the system.

13.1. CIRCUIT DIAGRAM

Connect all the components to Arduino as per the connections as described-

1. Temperature sensor analog out pin is connected to A0 pin of Arduino Uno.
2. 10K POT variable out pin is connected to A1 pin of Arduino Uno.
3. +Vcc and Ground pin of individual sensors is connected to +5V and GND pin of power Patch/explorer.

Rajesh Singh, Anita Gehlot, Bhupendra Singh & Sushabhan Choudhury
All rights reserved-© 2018 Bentham Science Publishers

4. DC jack of +12 V power supply is connected to power supply DC jack of Arduino mega.

5. Input pins 2 and 7 of L293D IC are connected to 10 and 9 pins of Arduino Uno to supply the input.

6. Output pins 3 and 8 of L293D IC are connected to +ve and –ve terminals of DC motor.

7. +12V and ground of power supply is connected to H bridge Collector and Emitter.

8. LEDs are also connected parallel to inputs of H -bridge.

9. +12V DC jack of power supply is connected to DC jack of Arduino Uno.

10. Pins 1,9 and 16 of L293D are connected to +5V.

11. Pins 4,5 and 12 ,13 are connected to ground.

Fig. (**13.2**) shows circuit diagram for the system.

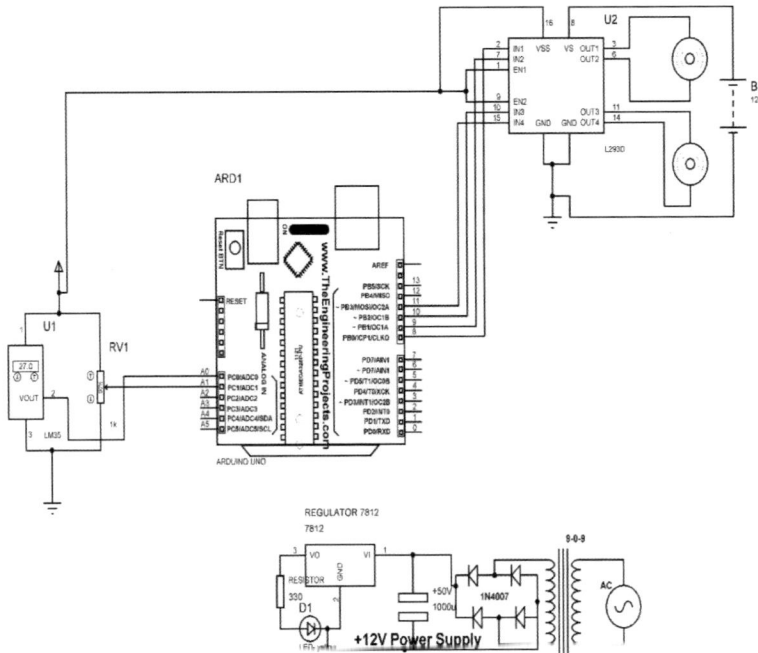

Fig. (**13.2**). Circuit diagram for the system.

13.2. MATLAB GUI

Create MATLAB GUI as described in chapter 7 and write program and functions to access data on created GUI. Burn the code for ADIOES to Arduino.

Program

```
function varargout = READ_WRITE_ADIOES(varargin)

gui_Singleton = 1;

gui_State = struct('gui_Name',        mfilename, ...
                   'gui_Singleton', gui_Singleton, ...
                   'gui_OpeningFcn', @READ_WRITE_ADIOES_OpeningFcn, ...
                   'gui_OutputFcn', @READ_WRITE_ADIOES_OutputFcn, ...
                   'gui_LayoutFcn', [] , ...
                   'gui_Callback', []);
if nargin && ischar(varargin{1})
    gui_State.gui_Callback = str2func(varargin{1});
end

if nargout
    [varargout{1:nargout}] = gui_mainfcn(gui_State, varargin{:});
else
    gui_mainfcn(gui_State, varargin{:});
end

function READ_WRITE_ADIOES_OpeningFcn(hObject, eventdata, handles, varargin)

handles.output = hObject;

guidata(hObject, handles);

delete(instrfind({'Port'},{'COM2'}))

clear a;
```

```
global a;

global stop;

stop='e';

global entry;

entry=1;

global time;

time=0;

a = arduino('COM2');

a.pinMode(8, 'output');

a.pinMode(9, 'output');

a.pinMode(10, 'output');

a.pinMode(11, 'output');


function varargout = READ_WRITE_ADIOES_OutputFcn(hObject, eventdata, handles)

varargout{1} = handles.output;


function pushbutton1_Callback(hObject, eventdata, handles)

global k a

global entry;

x=0;y=0;z=0;w=0;

while (1)

    b=a.analogRead(0);

  c=a.analogRead(1);
```

```
d=a.analogRead(2);

e=a.analogRead(3);


b=b/2;

c=c/2;

d=d/2;

e=e/2;


x=[x,b];y =[y,c];z =[z,d];w =[w,e]

subplot(2,2,1);

  plot(x,'r'); grid on;drawnow;

pause(0.01);


subplot(2,2,2);

plot(y,'k');drawnow;grid on;

pause(0.01);

end

function edit1_Callback(hObject, eventdata, handles)

handles.data1=get(hObject,'String');

handles.xSamples=str2double(handles.data1);

guidata(hObject,handles);

function edit1_CreateFcn(hObject, eventdata, handles)

if ispc && isequal(get(hObject,'BackgroundColor'), get(0,'defaultUicontrolBack-
groundColor'))
```

```matlab
    set(hObject,'BackgroundColor','white');
end

function pushbutton4_Callback(hObject, eventdata, handles)
global a;
a.digitalWrite(8,1);
global a;
a.digitalWrite(9,0);
global a;
a.digitalWrite(10,1);
global a;
a.digitalWrite(11,0);
function pushbutton5_Callback(hObject, eventdata, handles)
global a;
a.digitalWrite(8,0);
global a;
a.digitalWrite(9,0);
global a;
a.digitalWrite(10,1);
global a;
a.digitalWrite(11,0);

function pushbutton6_Callback(hObject, eventdata, handles)
global a;
a.digitalWrite(8,1);
```

```matlab
global a;

a.digitalWrite(9,0);

global a;

a.digitalWrite(10,0);

global a;

a.digitalWrite(11,0);


function pushbutton7_Callback(hObject, eventdata, handles)

global a;

a.digitalWrite(8,0);

global a;

a.digitalWrite(9,1);

global a;

a.digitalWrite(10,0);

global a;

a.digitalWrite(11,1);

function pushbutton8_Callback(hObject, eventdata, handles)

a.digitalWrite(8,0);

global a;

a.digitalWrite(9,0);

global a;

a.digitalWrite(10,0);

global a;

a.digitalWrite(11,0);
```

function STOP_Callback(hObject, eventdata, handles)

global stop;

stop='e';

fclose(instrfind);

Fig. (**13.3**) shows the MATLAB GUI for the system.

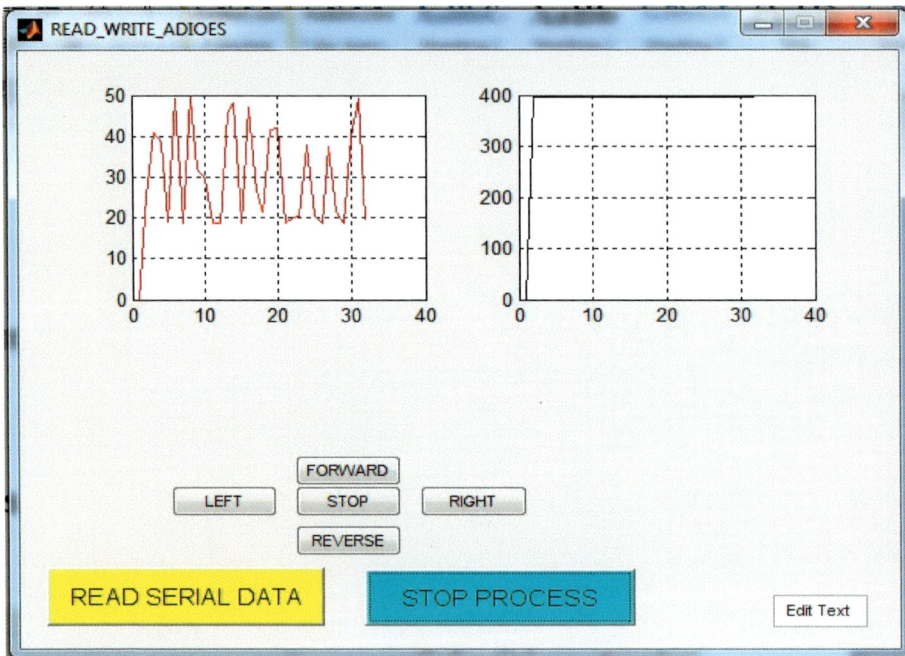

Fig. (13.3). MATLAB GUI.

CHAPTER 14

Two Analog Sensors [POT and LM35] Interfacing with Arduino I/O Package

Abstract: This chapter describes two analog sensors interfacing and data acquisition system with MATLAB. The system, comprises of Arduino board, LM35, POT, LED and power supply. The system is designed to receive two analog sensor data and control the LED.

Keywords : Analog sensor, Arduino, Arduino I/O package, LM35, POT.

Fig. (**14.1**) shows the block diagram of the system, comprises of Arduino board, LM35, POT, LED and power supply.

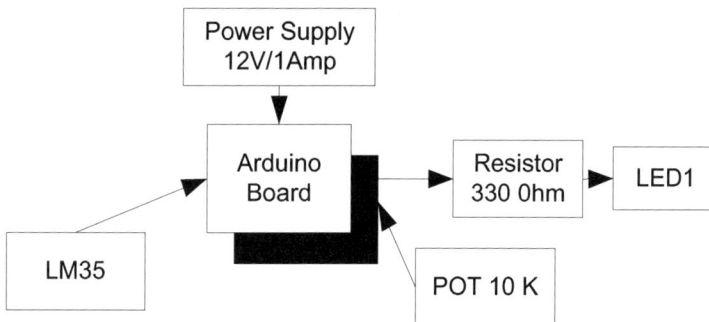

Fig. (14.1). Block diagram for interfacing of two analog sensors with Arduino with I/O package.

14.1. CIRCUIT DIAGRAM

Connect all the components to Arduino as per the connections as described-

1. Temperature sensor analog out pin is connected to A0 pin of Arduino Uno.
2. Temperature sensor analog out pin is connected to A1 pin of Arduino Uno.
3. LED D1 is connected with 8 pin of Arduino mega which is indicator through 330 ohm resistor.
4. +Vcc and Ground pin of individual sensors is connected to +5V and GND pin of power Patch/explorer.

Rajesh Singh, Anita Gehlot, Bhupendra Singh & Sushabhan Choudhury
All rights reserved-© 2018 Bentham Science Publishers

5. DC jack of +12 V power supply is connected to power supply DC jack of Arduino mega.

Fig. (**14.2**) shows circuit diagram for interfacing two analog sensors with Arduino with I/O package.

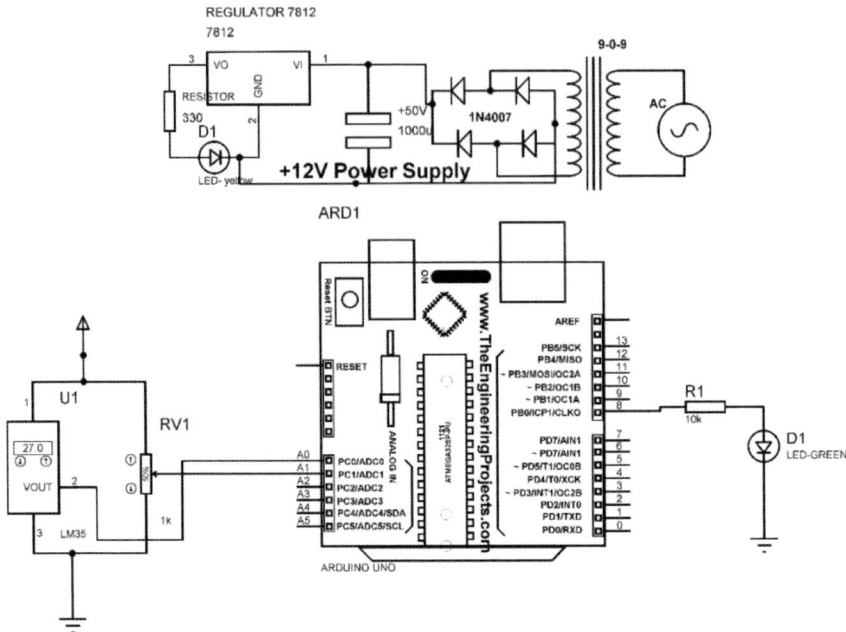

Fig. (**14.2**). Circuit diagram for interfacing of two analog sensors with Arduino with I/O package.

14.2. MATLAB GUI

Write program for MATLAB and develop GUI by following the steps in chapter 7.

Program

function varargout = Example1(varargin)

gui_Singleton = 1;

gui_State = struct('gui_Name', mfilename, ...

         'gui_Singleton', gui_Singleton, ...

         'gui_OpeningFcn', @Example1_OpeningFcn, ...

```matlab
          'gui_OutputFcn', @Example1_OutputFcn, ...

          'gui_LayoutFcn', [] , ...

          'gui_Callback', []);
if nargin && ischar(varargin{1})

   gui_State.gui_Callback = str2func(varargin{1});

end

if nargout

   [varargout{1:nargout}] = gui_mainfcn(gui_State, varargin{:});

else

   gui_mainfcn(gui_State, varargin{:});

end

function Example1_OpeningFcn(hObject, eventdata, handles, varargin)

handles.output = hObject;


guidata(hObject, handles);

delete(instrfind({'Port'},{'COM2'}))

clear a;

global a;

global stop;

stop='e';

global entry;

entry=1;

global time;

time=0;
```

```
a = arduino('COM2');

a.pinMode(8, 'output');

function varargout = Example1_OutputFcn(hObject, eventdata, handles)

varargout{1} = handles.output;

function turn_on_button_Callback(hObject, eventdata, handles)

global a;

a.digitalWrite(8,1);

function turn_off_button_Callback(hObject, eventdata, handles)

global a;

a.digitalWrite(8,0);

function read_button_Callback(hObject, eventdata, handles)

global k a

global entry;

x=0;y=0;

while (1)

    b=a.analogRead(0);

    c=a.analogRead(1);

    b=b/2;

    c=c/2;

    x=[x,b];y = [y,c];

      subplot(2,2,1);
```

```
   plot(x,'r'); grid on;drawnow;

  pause(0.01);

  subplot(2,2,2);

  plot(y,'k');drawnow;grid on;

  pause(0.01);


end

function edit_text_samples_Callback(hObject, eventdata, handles)

handles.data1=get(hObject,'String');

handles.xSamples=str2double(handles.data1);

guidata(hObject,handles);


function edit_text_samples_CreateFcn(hObject, eventdata, handles)

if ispc && isequal(get(hObject,'BackgroundColor'), get(0,'defaultUicontrolBack-
groundColor'))

   set(hObject,'BackgroundColor','white');

end

function stop_Callback(hObject, eventdata, handles)

global stop;

stop='e';

fclose(instrfind);
```

Fig. (**14.3**) shows the MATLAB GUI to read two analog sensors sensor with I/O package.

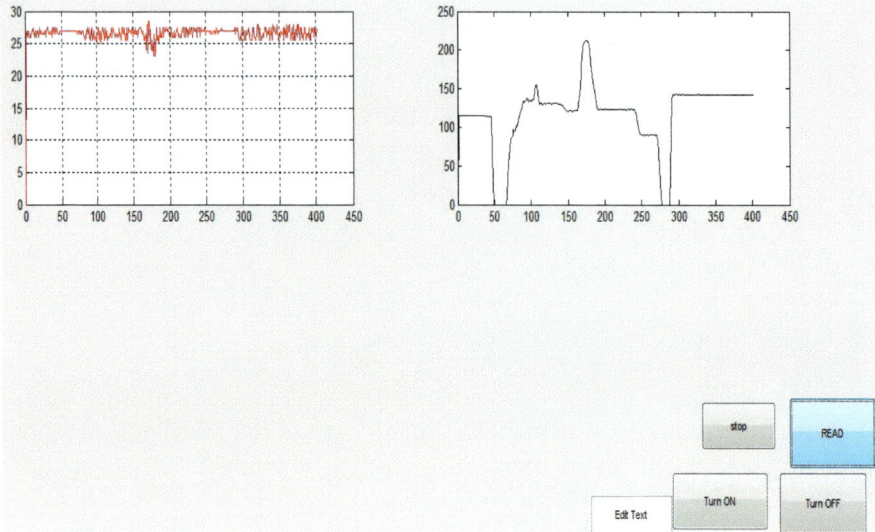

Fig. (14.3). MATLAB GUI to read two analog sensors sensor with I/O package.

CHAPTER 15

Three Sensors Data Acquisition and Feedback System with MATLAB and Arduino I/O Package

Abstract: This chapter explores the data acquisition and feedback system for three sensors with MATLAB and Arduino I/O package. The system comprises of Arduino board (connected to MATLAB GUI through serial), three sensors (LM35 (temperature), two POT (10K)) which are connected to Arduino, LED(output device) and power supply. The system is designed to receive the sensory data and control the LED with blocks created on MATLAB GUI.

Keywords: Arduino, Arduino GUI, LED, MATLAB GUI, POT, Temperature Sensor.

Fig. (**15.1**) shows the block diagram for the system which comprises of Arduino board (connected to MATLAB GUI through serial), three sensors (LM35 (temperature), two POT (10K)) which are connected to Arduino, LED(output device) and power supply.

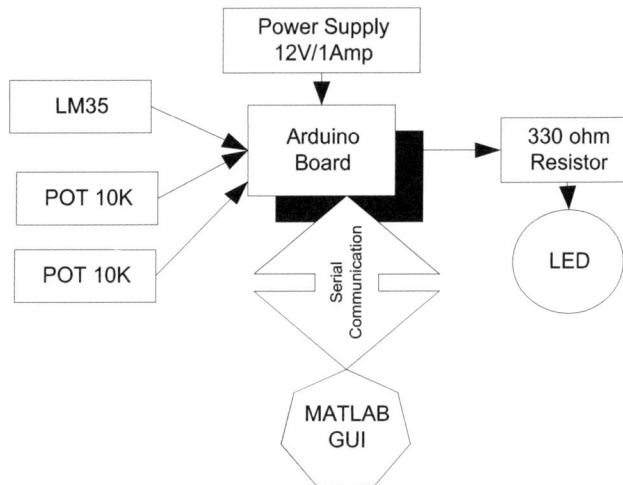

Fig. (15.1). Block diagram for interfacing of three sensors with Arduino with I/O package.

Rajesh Singh, Anita Gehlot, Bhupendra Singh & Sushabhan Choudhury
All rights reserved-© 2018 Bentham Science Publishers

15.1. CIRCUIT DIAGRAM

Connect all the components to Arduino as per the connections as described-

1. Temperature sensor analog out pin is connected to A0 pin of Arduino Uno.
2. 10K POT variable out pin is connected to A1 pin of Arduino Uno.
3. 10K POT variable out pin is connected to A2 pin of Arduino Uno.
4. +Vcc and Ground pin of individual sensors is connected to +5V and GND pin of power Patch/explorer.
5. DC jack of +12 V power supply is connected to power supply DC jack of Arduino Uno.
6. LED is connected to pin 8 of Arduino Uno.

Fig. (**15.2**) shows Circuit diagram for interfacing of three sensors with Arduino with I/O package.

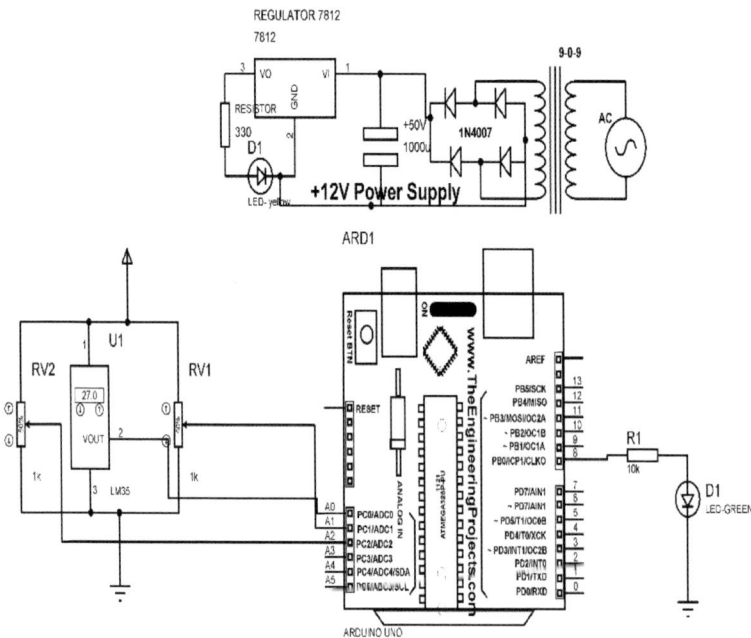

Fig. (15.2). Circuit diagram for interfacing of three sensors with Arduino with I/O package.

15.2. MATLAB GUI

Write program for MATLAB and develop GUI by following the steps in chapter 7.

Program

```
function varargout = channelread(varargin)

gui_Singleton = 1;

gui_State = struct('gui_Name', mfilename, ...
            'gui_Singleton', gui_Singleton, ...
            'gui_OpeningFcn', @channelread_OpeningFcn, ...
            'gui_OutputFcn', @channelread_OutputFcn, ...
            'gui_LayoutFcn', [] , ...
            'gui_Callback', []);

if nargin && ischar(varargin{1})
    gui_State.gui_Callback = str2func(varargin{1});
end

if nargout
    [varargout{1:nargout}] = gui_mainfcn(gui_State, varargin{:});
else
    gui_mainfcn(gui_State, varargin{:});
end

function channelread_OpeningFcn(hObject, eventdata, handles, varargin)

handles.output = hObject;

guidata(hObject, handles);

delete(instrfind({'Port'},{'COM2'}))

clear a;

global a;

global stop;
```

```
stop='e';

global entry;

entry=1;

global time;

time=0;

a = arduino('COM2');

a.pinMode(13, 'output');

function varargout = channelread_OutputFcn(hObject, eventdata, handles)

varargout{1} = handles.output;

function pushbutton1_Callback(hObject, eventdata, handles)

global a;

x=0;

while (1)

    b=a.analogRead(0);

    x=[x,b];

    plot(x);

    grid on;drawnow;

        pause(0.01);

end

function pushbutton2_Callback(hObject, eventdata, handles)

global a;

y=0;

while (1)

    c=a.analogRead(1);
```

```
    y=[y,c];

    plot(y,'r');

    grid on;drawnow;

      pause(0.01);

end

function pushbutton3_Callback(hObject, eventdata, handles)

delete(instrfind({'Port'},{'COM2'}))

function pushbutton4_Callback(hObject, eventdata, handles)

global a;

a.digitalWrite(10,1);

function pushbutton5_Callback(hObject, eventdata, handles)

global a;

a.digitalWrite(10,0);

function pushbutton7_Callback(hObject, eventdata, handles)

global a;

z=0;

while (1)

  e=a.analogRead(2);

  z=[z,e];

  plot(z,'g');

  grid on;drawnow;

    pause(0.01);

end
```

Fig. (**15.3**), (**15.4**) & (**15.5**) shows the MATLAB GUI for channel1, 2 & 3 respectively.

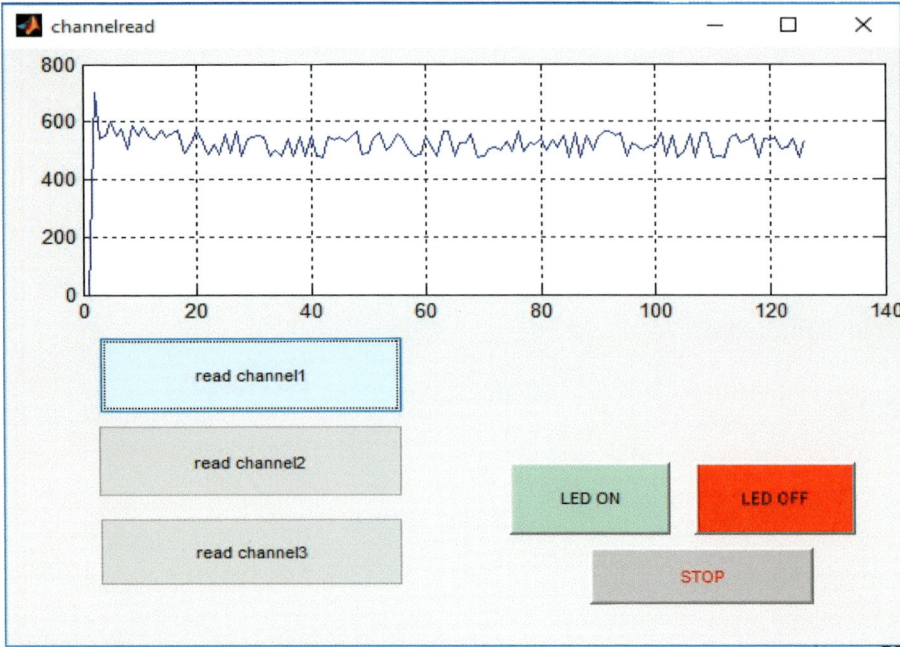

Fig. (15.3). MATLAB GUI showing channel 1 data.

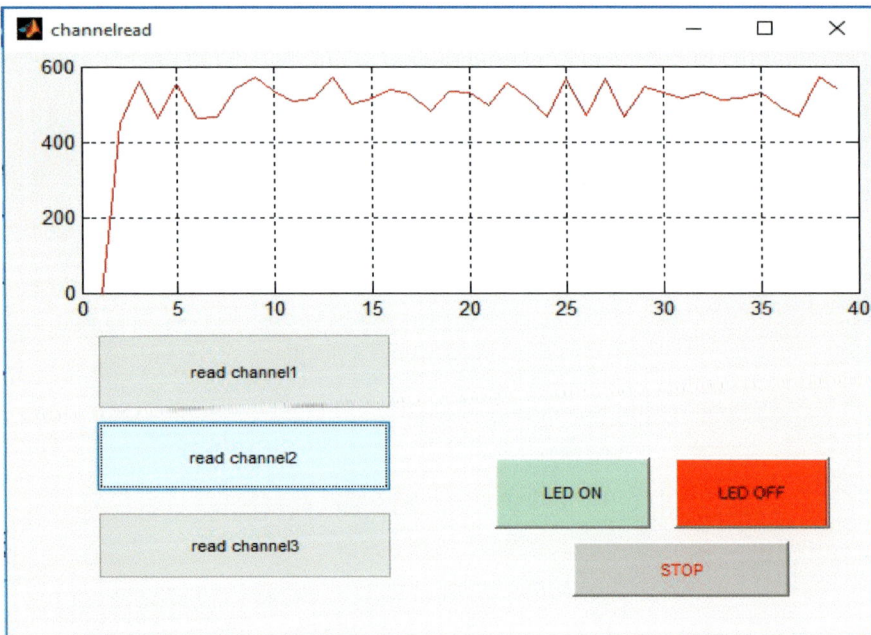

Fig. (15.4). MATLAB GUI showing channel2 data.

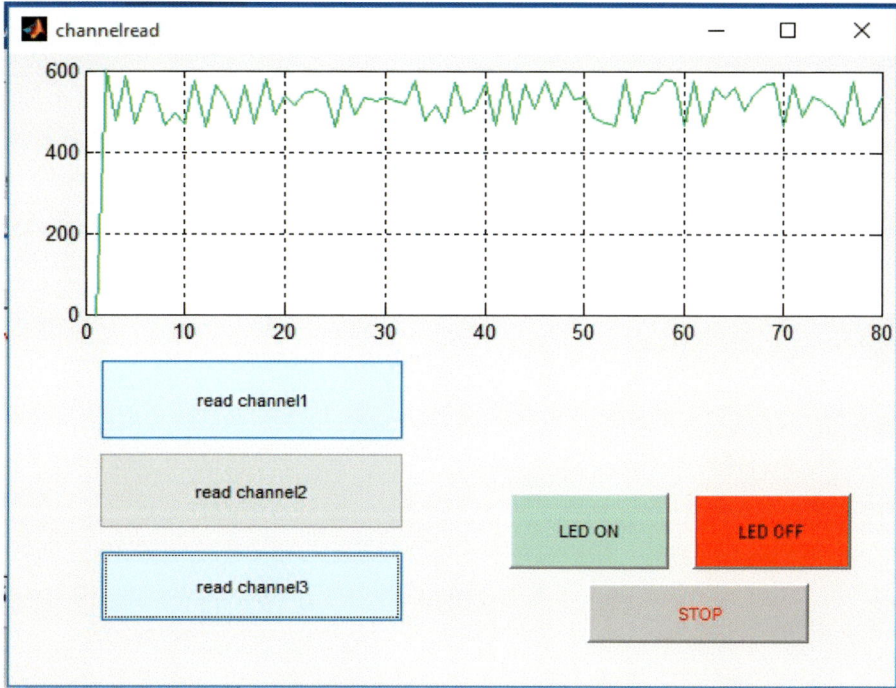

Fig. (15.5). MATLAB GUI showing channel3 data.

CHAPTER 16

Building Automation System

Abstract: This chapter describes the building automaton system with MATLAB. The system comprises of Arduino board (connected to MATLAB GUI through serial), four home appliances Bulb1, Fan1, Bulb2, Fan2, relay which are connected to Arduino through transistor and relay, and power supply. The system is designed to control appliances with blocks created on MATLAB GUI.

Keywords: Arduino, Bulb, Fan, GUI, MATLAB.

Fig. (**16.1**) show the block diagram for the system which comprises of Arduino board (connected to MATLAB GUI through serial), four home appliances (Bulb1, Fan1, Bulb2, Fan2, relay which are connected to Arduino through transistor and relay, and power supply.

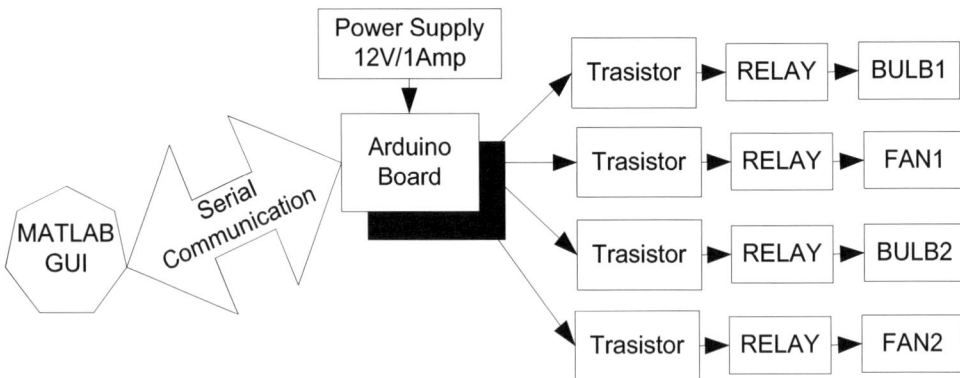

Fig. (16.1). Block diagram for building automation system.

16.1. CIRCUIT DIAGRAM

Connect all the components to Arduino as per the connections as described-

1. Pins 5,4,3 and 2 of Arduino are connected to pin IN_1, IN_2, IN_3 and IN_4 of RELAY board respectively.
2. Pin12 of Arduino is connected to pin RS of LCD.
3. Pin11 of Arduino is connected to pin E of LCD.

Rajesh Singh, Anita Gehlot, Bhupendra Singh & Sushabhan Choudhury
All rights reserved-© 2018 Bentham Science Publishers

4. Pin10 of Arduino is connected to pin D4 of LCD.
5. Pin9 of Arduino is connected to pin D5 of LCD.
6. Pin8 of Arduino is connected to pin D6 of LCD.
7. Pin7 of Arduino is connected to pin D7 of LCD.
8. GND of Arduino is connected to pin RW of LCD
9. +12V DC jack of power supply is connected to DC jack of Arduino.

Fig. (**16.2**) shows circuit diagram for building automation system.

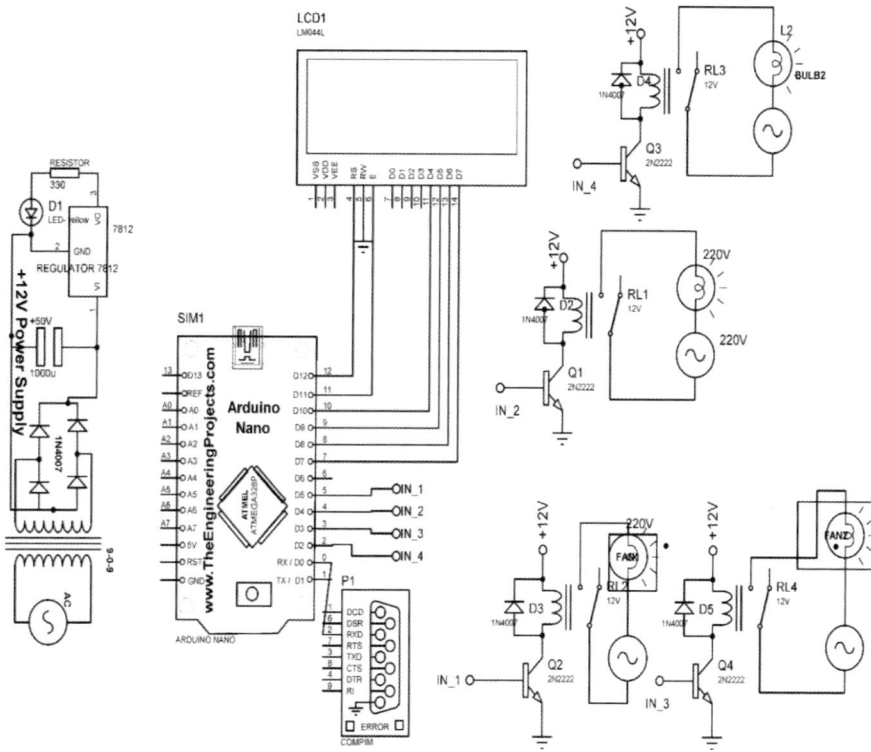

Fig. (16.2). Circuit diagram for building automation system.

16.2. PROGRAM

#include <LiquidCrystal.h>

LiquidCrystal lcd(12, 11, 10, 9, 8, 7);

const int M1_FAN1=5;

const int M1_BULB1=4;

```
const int M2_FAN2=3;

const int M2_BULB2=2;

int SERIAL_VAL;

void setup()
     {
     Serial.begin(9600);
     lcd.begin(20,4);
     pinMode(M1_FAN1, OUTPUT);
     pinMode(M1_BULB1, OUTPUT);
     pinMode(M2_FAN2, OUTPUT);
     pinMode(M2_BULB2, OUTPUT);
     lcd.setCursor(0,0);
     lcd.print("ROBOT");
     lcd.setCursor(0,1);
     lcd.print("CONTROL");
     delay(2000);
     }

void loop()
     {
if(Serial.available()>0)
     {
         SERIAL_VAL=Serial.read();

         if (SERIAL_VAL == 100)
```

```
    {

    lcd.clear();

    digitalWrite(M1_FAN1, HIGH);

    digitalWrite(M1_BULB1, LOW);

    digitalWrite(M1_FAN2, HIGH);

    digitalWrite(M1_BULB2, LOW);

    lcd.setCursor(0,0);

    lcd.print("FORWARD");

    delay(20);

    }

if(SERIAL_VAL == 101) // If use will send value 101 from MATLAB
then LED will turn OFF

    {

      lcd.clear();

digitalWrite(M1_FAN1, LOW);

digitalWrite(M1_BULB1, HIGH);

digitalWrite(M1_FAN2, LOW);

digitalWrite(M1_BULB2, HIGH);

 lcd.setCursor(0,1);

lcd.print("REVERSE");

delay(20);

}

if(SERIAL_VAL == 102) // If use will send value 101 from MATLAB
then LED will turn OFF
```

```
{

lcd.clear();

digitalWrite(M1_FAN1, HIGH);

digitalWrite(M1_BULB1, LOW);

digitalWrite(M1_FAN2, LOW);

digitalWrite(M1_BULB2, LOW);

lcd.setCursor(0,2);

lcd.print("LEFT ");

delay(20);

}

if(SERIAL_VAL == 103) // If use will send value 101 from MATLAB
then LED will turn OFF

{

lcd.clear();

digitalWrite(M1_FAN1, LOW);

digitalWrite(M1_BULB1, LOW);

digitalWrite(M1_FAN2, HIGH);

digitalWrite(M1_BULB2, LOW);

lcd.setCursor(0,3);

lcd.print("RIGHT ");

delay(20);

}

if(SERIAL_VAL == 104) // If use will send value 101 from MATLAB
then LED will turn OFF

{
```

```
        lcd.clear();

        digitalWrite(M1_FAN1, LOW);

        digitalWrite(M1_BULB1, LOW);

        digitalWrite(M1_FAN2, LOW);

        digitalWrite(M1_BULB2, LOW);

        lcd.setCursor(0,0);

        lcd.print("STOP ");

        delay(20);

        }

}

}
```

16.3. MATLAB GUI

Write program for MATLAB and develop GUI by following the steps in chapter 7.

Program

```
function varargout = AUTOMATION_4_appliances(varargin)

gui_Singleton = 1;

gui_State = struct('gui_Name', mfilename, ...

            'gui_Singleton', gui_Singleton, ...

            'gui_OpeningFcn', @AUTOMATION_4_appliances_OpeningFcn, ...

            'gui_OutputFcn', @AUTOMATION_4_appliances_OutputFcn, ...

            'gui_LayoutFcn', [] , ...

            'gui_Callback', []);
```

```
if nargin && ischar(varargin{1})

gui_State.gui_Callback = str2func(varargin{1});

end


if nargout

    [varargout{1:nargout}] = gui_mainfcn(gui_State, varargin{:});

else

    gui_mainfcn(gui_State, varargin{:});

end


function    AUTOMATION_4_appliances_OpeningFcn(hObject,    eventdata,
handles, varargin)

handles.output = hObject;


guidata(hObject, handles);

function  varargout  =  AUTOMATION_4_appliances_OutputFcn(hObject,
eventdata, handles)

handles.output = hObject;

varargout{1} = handles.output;


function FAN1_Callback(hObject, eventdata, handles)

fprintf(handles.s,100);

handles.output = hObject;

guidata(hObject, handles);

function FAN2_Callback(hObject, eventdata, handles)

fprintf(handles.s,102);

handles.output = hObject;
```

```
guidata(hObject, handles);

function BULB1_Callback(hObject, eventdata, handles)
fprintf(handles.s,101);
handles.output = hObject;
guidata(hObject, handles);
function BULB2_Callback(hObject, eventdata, handles)

fprintf(handles.s,103);
handles.output = hObject;
guidata(hObject, handles);

function START_Callback(hObject, eventdata, handles)
handles.output = hObject;
global s;
handles.s=s;
handles.s=serial('COM2','BAUD', 9600);
fopen(handles.s);
guidata(hObject, handles);

function EXIT_Callback(hObject, eventdata, handles)
delete(instrfind({'Port'},{'COM2'}));
close all;
```

Fig. (**16.3**) shows MATLAB GUI for building automation.

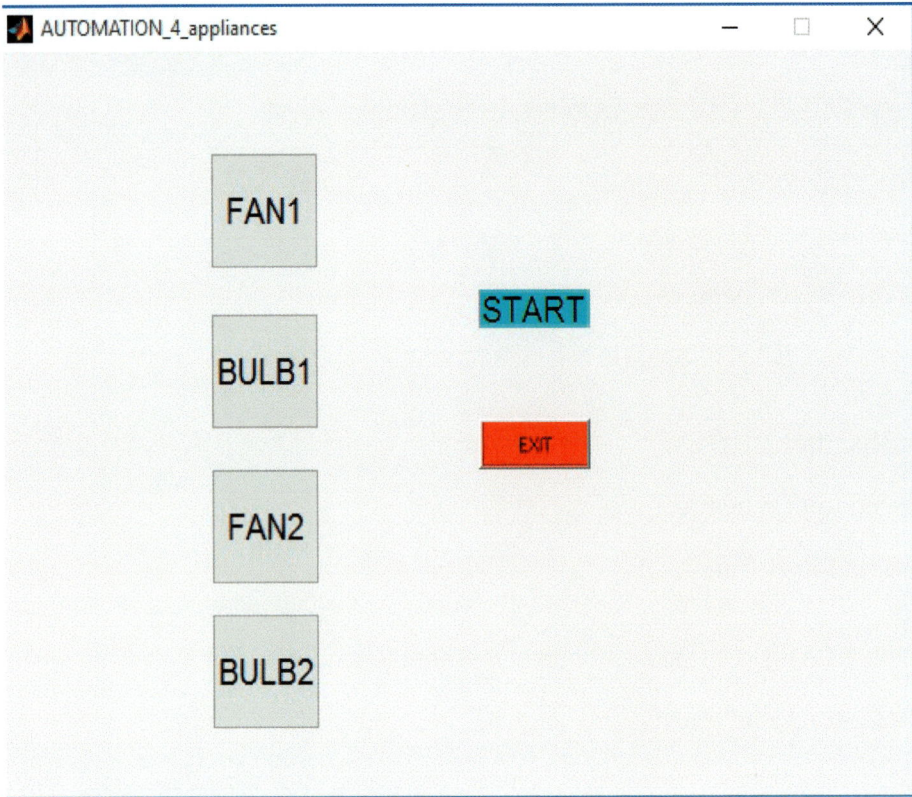

Fig. (16.3). MATLAB GUI for building automation.

CHAPTER 17

Robot Control with MATLAB GUI

Abstract: This chapter describes the robot control with MATLAB. The system comprises of Arduino board (connected to MATLAB GUI through serial), four robot control (motor1, motor2) which are connected to Arduino through L293D, and power supply. The system is designed to control robot with blocks created on MATLAB GUI.

Keywords: Arduino, GUI, L293D, MATLAB, Motor, Robot.

Fig. (**17.1**) show the block diagram for the system which comprises of Arduino board (connected to MATLAB GUI through serial), four robot control (motor1, motor2) which are connected to Arduino through L293D, and power supply.

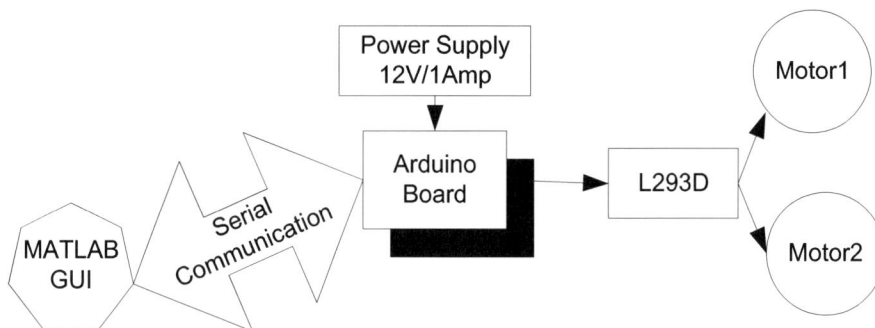

Fig. (17.1). Block diagram for robot control with MATLAB GUI.

17.1. CIRCUIT DIAGRAM

Connect all the components to Arduino as per the connections as described-

1. Pins 2,7,10 and 15 of L293Dare connected to pin 5,4,3,2 of Arduino Nano respectively.
2. Output of L293D 3,6,11 and 14 are connected to pin +ve and –ve of Motor1 and +ve and –ve of motor 2 respectively.
3. Pin12 of Arduino is connected to pin RS of LCD.
4. Pin11 of Arduino is connected to pin E of LCD.

Rajesh Singh, Anita Gehlot, Bhupendra Singh & Sushabhan Choudhury
All rights reserved-© 2018 Bentham Science Publishers

5. Pin10 of Arduino is connected to pin D4 of LCD.
6. Pin9 of Arduino is connected to pin D5 of LCD.
7. Pin8 of Arduino is connected to pin D6 of LCD.
8. Pin7 of Arduino is connected to pin D7 of LCD.
9. GND of Arduino is connected to pin RW of LCD
10. +12V DC jack of power supply is connected to DC jack of Arduino.

Fig. (**17.2**) shows circuit diagram for robot control with MATLAB GUI.

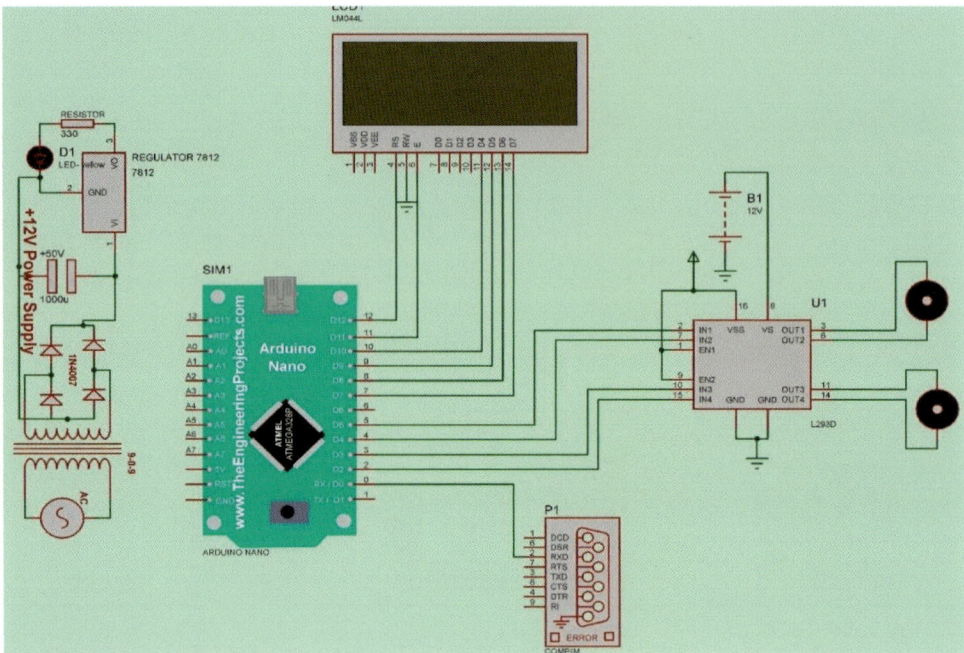

Fig. (17.2). Circuit diagram for robot control with MATLAB GUI.

17.2. PROGRAM

#include <LiquidCrystal.h>

LiquidCrystal lcd(12, 11, 10, 9, 8, 7);

const int M1_POS=5;

const int M1_NEG=4;

const int M2_POS=3;

const int M2_NEG=2;

```
int SERIAL_VAL;

void setup()
    {
    Serial.begin(9600);
    lcd.begin(20,4);
    pinMode(M1_POS, OUTPUT);
    pinMode(M1_NEG, OUTPUT);
    pinMode(M2_POS, OUTPUT);
    pinMode(M2_NEG, OUTPUT);
    lcd.setCursor(0,0);
    lcd.print("ROBOT");
    lcd.setCursor(0,1);
    lcd.print("CONTROL");
    delay(2000);
    }

void loop()
    {
    if(Serial.available()>0)
    {
      SERIAL_VAL=Serial.read();

     if (SERIAL_VAL == 100)
       {
       lcd.clear();
```

```
digitalWrite(M1_POS, HIGH);

digitalWrite(M1_NEG, LOW);

digitalWrite(M1_POS, HIGH);

digitalWrite(M1_POS, LOW);

lcd.setCursor(0,0);

lcd.print("FORWARD");

delay(20);

}


if(SERIAL_VAL == 101) // If use will send value 101 from MATLAB
then LED will turn OFF

{

lcd.clear();

digitalWrite(M1_POS, LOW);

digitalWrite(M1_NEG, HIGH);

digitalWrite(M1_POS, LOW);

digitalWrite(M1_POS, HIGH);

lcd.setCursor(0,1);

lcd.print("REVERSE");

delay(20);

}

if(SERIAL_VAL == 102) // If use will send value 101 from MATLAB
then LED will turn OFF

{

lcd.clear();
```

```
digitalWrite(M1_POS, HIGH);

digitalWrite(M1_NEG, LOW);

digitalWrite(M1_POS, LOW);

digitalWrite(M1_POS, LOW);

lcd.setCursor(0,2);

lcd.print("LEFT ");

delay(20);

}

if(SERIAL_VAL == 103) // If use will send value 101 from MATLAB
then LED will turn OFF

{

lcd.clear();

digitalWrite(M1_POS, LOW);

digitalWrite(M1_NEG, LOW);

digitalWrite(M1_POS, HIGH);

digitalWrite(M1_POS, LOW);

lcd.setCursor(0,3);

lcd.print("RIGHT ");

delay(20);

}

if(SERIAL_VAL == 104) // If use will send value 101 from MATLAB
then LED will turn OFF

{

lcd.clear();

digitalWrite(M1_POS, LOW);
```

```
    digitalWrite(M1_NEG, LOW);

    digitalWrite(M1_POS, LOW);

    digitalWrite(M1_POS, LOW);

    lcd.setCursor(0,0);

    lcd.print("STOP ");

    delay(20);

       }

  }

  }
```

17.3. MATLAB GUI

Write program for MATLAB and develop GUI by following the steps in chapter 7.

Program

```
function varargout = ROBOT_book_matlab(varargin)

gui_Singleton = 1;

gui_State = struct('gui_Name', mfilename, ...

             'gui_Singleton', gui_Singleton, ...

             'gui_OpeningFcn', @ROBOT_book_matlab_OpeningFcn, ...

             'gui_OutputFcn', @ROBOT_book_matlab_OutputFcn, ...

             'gui_LayoutFcn', [] , ...

             'gui_Callback', []);

if nargin && ischar(varargin{1})

   gui_State.gui_Callback = str2func(varargin{1});

end
```

```
if nargout

    [varargout{1:nargout}] = gui_mainfcn(gui_State, varargin{:});

else

    gui_mainfcn(gui_State, varargin{:});

end

function   ROBOT_book_matlab_OpeningFcn(hObject,   eventdata,   handles,
varargin)

handles.output = hObject;

guidata(hObject, handles);

function  varargout  =  ROBOT_book_matlab_OutputFcn(hObject,  eventdata,
handles)

varargout{1} = handles.output;


function FORWARD_Callback(hObject, eventdata, handles)

fprintf(handles.s,100);

handles.output = hObject;

guidata(hObject, handles);


function REVERSE_Callback(hObject, eventdata, handles)

fprintf(handles.s,101);

handles.output = hObject;

guidata(hObject, handles);


function LEFT_Callback(hObject, eventdata, handles)

fprintf(handles.s,102);

handles.output = hObject;
```

```
guidata(hObject, handles);

function RIGHT_Callback(hObject, eventdata, handles)

fprintf(handles.s,103);

handles.output = hObject;

guidata(hObject, handles);

function STOP_Callback(hObject, eventdata, handles)

fprintf(handles.s,104);

handles.output = hObject;

guidata(hObject, handles);


function START_Callback(hObject, eventdata, handles)

handles.output = hObject;

global s;

handles.s=s;

handles.s=serial('COM2','BAUD', 9600);

fopen(handles.s);

guidata(hObject, handles);

function EXIT_Callback(hObject, eventdata, handles)

delete(instrfind({'Port'},{'COM2'}));

close all;
```

Fig. (**17.3**) shows MATLAB GUI for robot control with MATLAB GUI.

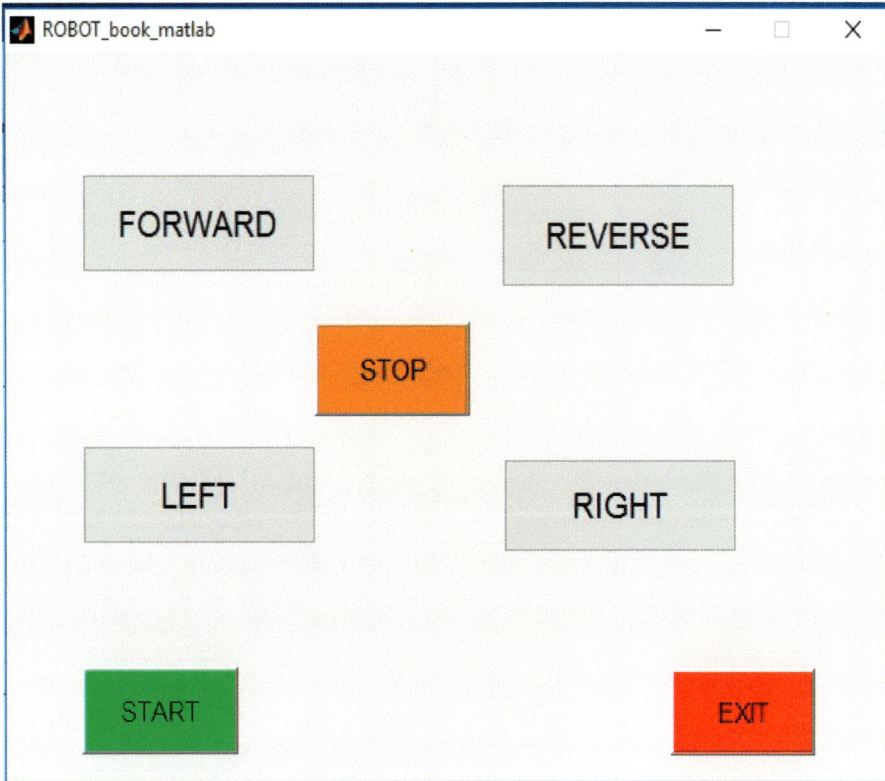

Fig. (17.3). MATLAB GUI for robot control with MATLAB GUI.

CHAPTER 18

One Analog Channel and Digital Write Using MATLAB GUI

Abstract: This chapter describes how to read one analog channel with MATLAB and output as digital write for controlling the device connected go it. The system comprises of Arduino board which is connected to MATLAB GUI through serial, POT, LED and power supply. The system will sense the change in POT and processed through MATLAB and send output to digital pin.

Keywords: Analog channel, Arduino, Digital write, GUI, MATLAB.

Fig. (**18.1**) shows the block diagram for the system, comprises of Arduino board which is connected to MATLAB GUI through serial, POT, LED and power supply.

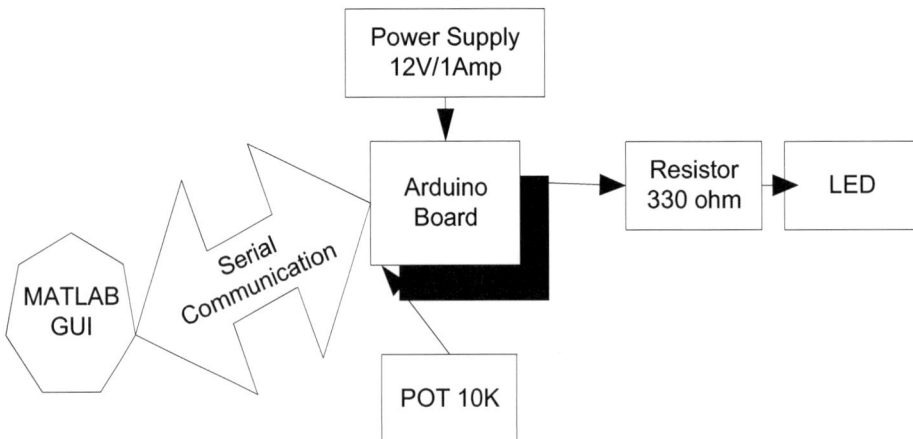

Fig. (**18.1**). Block diagram for one analog channel and digital write using MATLAB GUI.

18.1. CIRCUIT DIAGRAM

Connect all the components to Arduino as per the connections as described-

1. Variable terminal of POT of 10K is connected to A0 pin Arduino.

Rajesh Singh, Anita Gehlot, Bhupendra Singh & Sushabhan Choudhury
All rights reserved-© 2018 Bentham Science Publishers

2. Fixed terminals of POT is connected to +5V and GND of Power supply patch.
3. LED is connected to pin4 of Arduino through 330-ohm resistor.
4. +12V DC jack of power supply is connected to DC jack of Arduino.

Fig. (**18.2**) shows circuit diagram for one analog channel and digital write using MATLAB GUI.

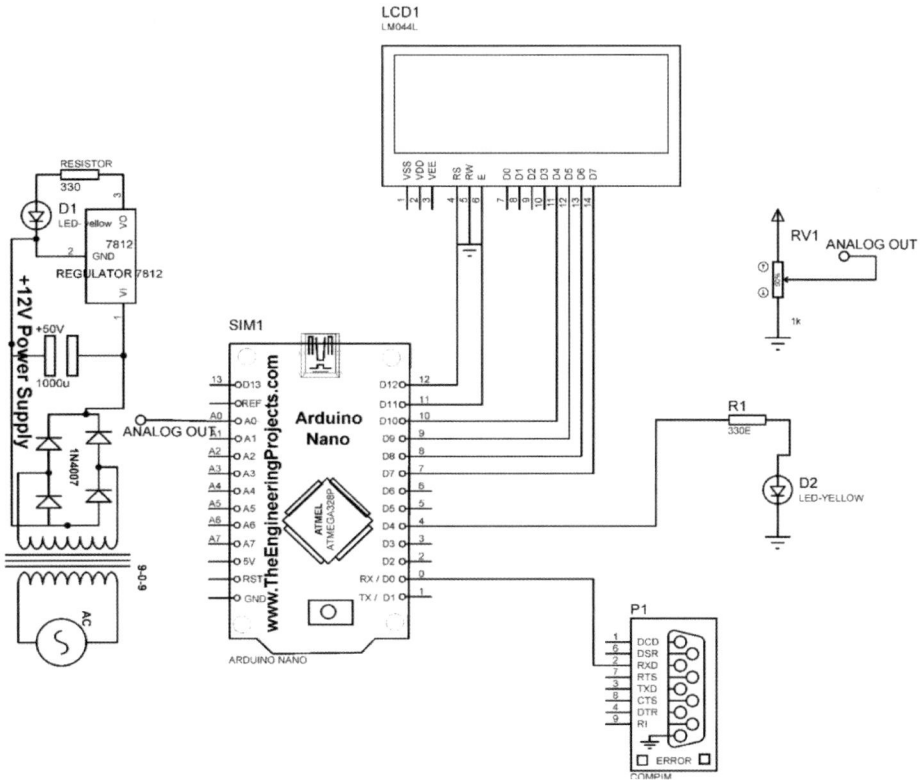

Fig. (**18.2**). Circuit diagram for one analog channel and digital write using MATLAB GUI.

18.2. PROGRAM

```
const int led_pin_OUTPUT=13;

int SERIAL_READ_DATA;

int adc_POT=0;

void setup()

{

Serial.begin(9600);
```

```
pinMode(led, OUTPUT);

}

void loop()

{

//// read analog sensor from arduino

adc_POT = analogRead(A0);

Serial.println(adc);

delay(200);


///// write to arduino

if(Serial.available()>0)

{

SERIAL_READ_DATA=Serial.read();

if (SERIAL_READ_DATA == 100)

{

digitalWrite(led_pin_OUTPUT, HIGH);

delay(10);

}

if(SERIAL_READ_DATA == 101)

{

digitalWrite(led_pin_OUTPUT, LOW);

delay(10);

}
```

```
}


}
```

18.3. MATLAB GUI

Write program for MATLAB and develop GUI by following the steps in chapter 7.

Program

```
function varargout = ledadcplot(varargin)

gui_Singleton = 1;

gui_State = struct('gui_Name', mfilename, ...

                'gui_Singleton', gui_Singleton, ...

                'gui_OpeningFcn', @ledadcplot_OpeningFcn, ...

                'gui_OutputFcn', @ledadcplot_OutputFcn, ...

                'gui_LayoutFcn', [] , ...

                'gui_Callback', []);

if nargin && ischar(varargin{1})

   gui_State.gui_Callback = str2func(varargin{1});

end


if nargout

   [varargout{1:nargout}] = gui_mainfcn(gui_State, varargin{:});

else

   gui_mainfcn(gui_State, varargin{:});

end

function ledadcplot_OpeningFcn(hObject, eventdata, handles, varargin)
```

```
handles.output = hObject;

guidata(hObject, handles);

global stop;
stop='x';
global entry;
entry=1;
global time;
time=0;
global s;
s = serial('COM2','BaudRate',9600);
fopen(s);

function varargout = ledadcplot_OutputFcn(hObject, eventdata, handles)

varargout{1} = handles.output;
function ON_Callback(hObject, eventdata, handles)
global s;
handles.s=s;
fprintf(handles.s,100);
handles.output = hObject;
guidata(hObject, handles);

function OFF_Callback(hObject, eventdata, handles)
global s;
handles.s=s;
```

```
fprintf(handles.s,101);

%fopen(handles.s);

handles.output = hObject;

guidata(hObject, handles);

function adc_Callback(hObject, eventdata, handles)

global s;

global stop;

global time;

time = 0;

global entry;

global logRange

logRange=100;

i =0;

while(1)

    i = i + 1;

    adc(i) = fscanf(s,'%d');

    drawnow;

    k= length(time);

    if (time(k))>100

    axes(handles.axes1);

    plot(time(k-logRange:k),adc(k-logRange:k),'r','LineWidth',2);xlim([time-
k-logRange) time(k)]);ylim([0 2000]);xlabel('Time'); ylabel('Amplitude');

    grid on;
```

else

axes(handles.axes1);   plot(time,adc,'r','LineWidth',2);ylim([0   2000]);
xlabel('Time'); ylabel('Amplitude'); grid; drawnow;

end

pause(.2);

time=[time,time(length(time))+1];

end

function stop_Callback(hObject, eventdata, handles)

delete(instrfind({'Port'},{'COM2'}));

close all;

Fig. (**18.3**) shows MATLAB GUI for one analog channel and digital write.

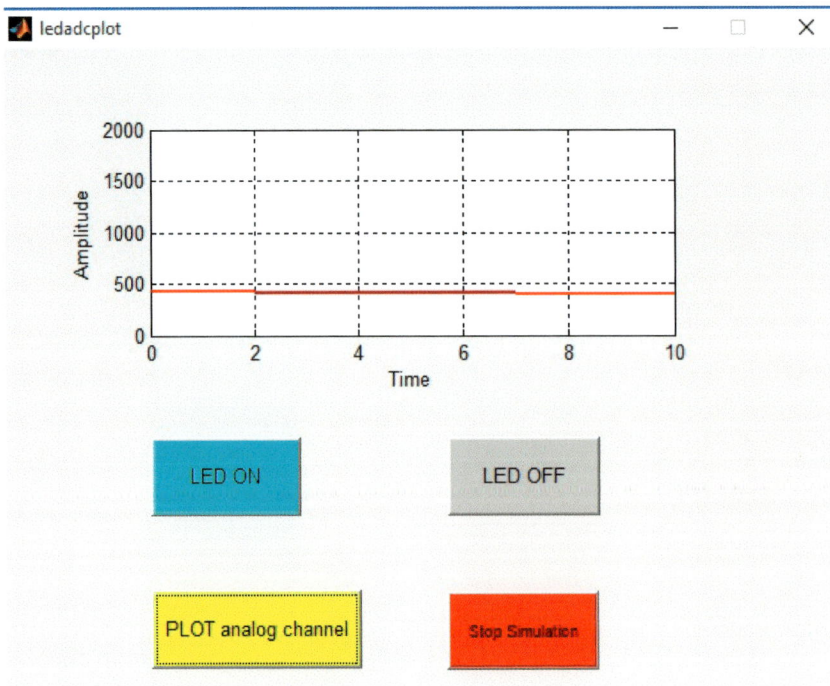

Fig. (18.3). MATLAB GUI for one analog channel and digital write.

BIBLIOGRAPHY

[1]   https://in.mathworks.com/help/matlab/creating_guis/about-the-simple-guide-gui-example.html?requestedDomain=true

[2]   https://www.arduino.cc/en/Main/Software

[3]   https://www.arduino.cc/en/Guide/Windows

[4]   http://ctms.engin.umich.edu/CTMS/index.php?aux=Activities_IOpack

[5]   R. Singh, A. Gehlot, B. Singh, and S. Choudhury, *"Arduino-Based Embedded Systems: Interfacing, Simulation, and LabVIEW GUI"- CRC Press.,* Taylor & Francis, . ISBN 9781138060784

[6]   R. Singh, A. Gehlot, S. Choudhury, and B. Singh, *Embedded System based on Atmega Microcontroller- Simulation, Interfacing and Projects.,* Narosa Publishing House, . ISBN: 978-8--8487-5720

[7]   P.S. Pandey, R. Singh, A. Gehlot, B. Singh, and S. Choudhury, *Power Line Carrier Communication and Arduino based Automation.,* RI Publication, . ISBN: 9780387374010

SUBJECT INDEX

Rajesh Singh, Anita Gehlot, Bhupendra Singh & Sushabhan Choudhury
All rights reserved-© 2018 Bentham Science Publishers

18197479R00089

Printed in Great Britain
by Amazon